THE MISSING LINK

Revealing Spiritual Genetics

Richard Gene Arno, Ph.D.
Phyllis Jean Arno, Ph.D.

the Peppertree Press

For thou hast possessed my reins:
thou has covered me
in my mother's womb.

I will praise thee; for I am
fearfully and wonderfully
made: marvellous are thy
works; and that my soul
knoweth right well.

Psalm 139:13-14

TABLE OF CONTENTS

FOREWORD
Temperament is Biblical!

by Dr. Gary W. Polston

When I was first introduced to the theory that is taught by the Arnos, the initial question I asked was whether or not temperament was taught in the Bible. The reply was: "The word temperament is not specifically used in the Bible; however, it is evidenced in the Beatitudes and many other places."

My early educational background was in the field of humanistic Clinical Psychology. After becoming a Christian I was introduced to "Christian Psychology" and attended a major Christian college for further study in this field. It didn't take long before I realized that "Christian Psychology" was an oxymoron. The professors were doing nothing more than trying to make the Word of God fit the teachings of godless men. Consequently, I realized that the answers to man's problems did not rest in the heretical teachings of Freud, B.F. Skinner, Carl Rogers, etc., but in God Himself. Hence I changed my major and continued my studies until I earned a Doctorate in Theology.

I entered into a quest, not to make the Bible fit the teaching of temperament, but to see if it was a genuine biblical precept. The following is a synopsis of my studies.

In Proverbs 22:6 the Bible says:

"Train up a child in the way he should go; and when he is old, he will not depart from it."

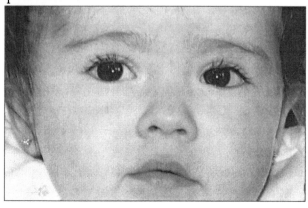

The popular interpretation of this verse espouses that if a believer will make his child go to Sunday school, church, Christian school, read his Bible, and teach him the same at home, when he grows into old age, he will ultimately return to God. As one who has been a follower of Jesus Christ for over thirty years, I would submit to you that this explanation is erroneous.

You and I know any number of rebels who were forced into a restricted, parent-dominated, externally religious lifestyle during their early years at home. When they got free from all that, they went wild and never did stop running away from God. In fact, they did not return to the Lord, even when they grew older. This Christian knows of some who died while running from the Lord. Likewise, I have spoken to more than a few elderly folks in their hour of death who were raised in Christian homes and still would not accept Jesus Christ as their Savior.

As a pastor and counselor, I have witnessed many parents of adult children who have either been told that they failed to bring their child up in the "nurture and admonition of the Lord" (Ephesians 6:4), or that they essentially failed as parents. These parents reside in guilt. The insight that a teenager or an adult child has a free will to accept or reject Jesus Christ as Savior, just as their parents did, never seems to enter into the picture. This grown child is a free moral agent and personally responsible for his or her own choices.

This popular interpretation will not hold water exegetically. The precept taught in this verse is found in two Hebrew words. The first is peh, translated "he should go" which has to do with the palate of an infant's mouth. When the mother's breast is pressed against the palate of a newborn's mouth, it triggers a sucking response. The teaching from peh is for the parent to "create a hunger" in the child. We are to create a hunger in our children to pursue a specific direction that will inspire them throughout their entire life.

The second word is derek, translated "way." "Some Hebrew scholars define "derek" as "a child's individual gift or bent." In the Greek Septuagint (Greek translation of the Old Testament), the word is phusikos orphusis, which is defined by the Greek scholars as "nature, constitution, temperament."

Therefore, the principle of Proverbs 22:6 is that we should "train up" (peh) or create a hunger in a child in the way that he should go, according to his God-given (phusis) temperament; then when he is old he will not depart from it. Why? Because it is the way God fearfully and wonderfully made him to be... his nature, his constitution, his temperament.

Hippocrates, the Greek physician called the father of modern medicine, began to do the first scientific research relating to phusies or temperament (HP.Acut.43; Hp.Fract.7; phusies nousoon ieetroi Hp.Epid. 6.5.1). He refers to phusis hundreds of times in his writings.

Likewise, other Greek scholars and philosophers such as Socrates and Plato made reference to phusis thousands of times throughout their writings. Plato taught his students about temperament in the Academy which he founded in 386 A.D. He alludes to phusis all through The Republic (Plat. Rep. 375b; 410e; 525c; 576a etc.).

Temperament has been studied scientifically longer than any other theory in the field confirms its validity for the believer. History proves that it has been scientifically investigated for thousands of years, beginning with Solomon (the writer of Proverbs). God has allowed Drs. Richard and Phyllis Arno to develop the theory of temperament and a personal temperament identification system called the Arno Profile System (A.P.S.). This profile system accurately determines an individual's temperament and enables us to understand ourselves.

The Arnos have probably done more to bring the scientific study of temperament to fruition than anyone thus far in history.

Introduction

Most high schools and colleges teach students about human behavior as a part of general psychology courses. Unfortunately, these general psychology courses are usually based on the assumption that man evolved from lower life forms.

As Christians, we believe that we were created by God. We believe that He created us for a divine purpose and that each and every person is unique.

Sigmund Freud believed that we are born a "blank slate" and that who we are and who we become is a grand summation of our human experiences, i.e., that we are a result of learned behavior. Even though Sigmund Freud's theory has been proven wrong, it is still taught as fact in most high schools and colleges.

Believing that humans evolved is not only wrong, it is extremely dangerous. It allows an individual to believe that he or she is not accountable. If we believe that we evolved, then we also believe that there is no god, no one to answer to and no eternal accountability for the life we live. Believing that we are simply a product of our experiences also allows us to pass the blame for our actions onto others. We can simply say, "It's my mother's fault." Or, "It's society's fault that I turned out this way."

This book teaches accountability for each individual's actions and helps the reader understand who God created him or her to be. It teaches how His wonderful plan, for us as individuals, works and how it can cause every person to be happy and fulfilled during this life.

Understanding human behavior helps us understand ourselves. It allows us to be the best that God has created us to be by meeting our needs in a way which is pleasing to Him.

Full and complete change of a human being is an act of God. It is imperative for you to realize that we do not want to teach, or even imply, that the application of this knowledge can change a human being. It is the understanding and acceptance of one's unique self which causes each individual to allow God to effect change in his/her life. This book encourages:

a. Understanding of one's unique self.
b. Surrendering to the Lord Jesus Christ and His plan for our lives.
c. A willingness to surrender the ungodly ways of meeting our temperament needs and replacing them with methods which are taught in the Holy Scriptures. This is a daily surrender.

Our temperament is placed within us by God, while in our mother's womb, and our temperament will remain with us throughout our lives. We are spiritual beings created by God with a precise order and balance of body, soul and spirit.

Our hearts are the binding, blending and balancing agents within our temperament. This overlaps our souls and spirits and provides God's precise order within each of us.

Every individual has temperament needs of varying degrees. These needs are met by drawing from the lower soul (humanistic) or from the higher soul, most commonly referred to as the spirit. Most interpersonal and intrapersonal conflicts are caused by:

a. Individuals attempting to meet their temperament needs in an ungodly way (drawing from the lower soul).
b. Temperament needs being out of balance, i.e., all the individual's energies spent meeting some needs while other needs are ignored.
c. Reactions to unmet temperament needs.

It is our prayer that having this new, Biblically-based knowledge about yourself and about general human behavior, will be a blessing to you and a source of a happy and fulfilling life.

What Is Temperament?

✤ 1 ✤

Temperament, in simple terms, is the inborn (not genetic, i.e., brown hair, blue eyes, etc.) part of man that determines how he reacts to people, places, and things. In short, it is how we interact with our environment and the world around us. Temperament pinpoints our perception of ourselves and the people who love us. It is also the determining factor in how well we handle the stresses and pressures of life. In essence, temperament is our spiritual genetics.

According to many secular psychologists, people are born as blank slates (tabula rasa). This school of thought originated with St. Thomas Aquinas (1225-1274) and was developed further by John Locke (1632-1704) and capitalized on by Sigmund Freud (1856-1939). The Neo-Freudians believe that the environment and developmental stages are

1

what determines man's behavior. Although there are effects from the environment and developmental stages, you cannot convince the parent of a newborn baby that his/her child is born a blank slate and has no unique behavior patterns.

Some newborns will coo sweetly, sleep long hours and cry only when wet or hungry. There are others who will awaken every couple of hours, scream at the top of their lungs and resist any efforts to be quieted. There are newborns who will cuddle and laugh for any adult who holds them, and there are some who are comfortable with no one but their mothers or fathers. This is the observable proof of temperament. If children were born blank you could see this when you look into a hospital nursery because the babies would all behave in the same way; yet, as you know, each infant is different.

Paul D. Meier, M.D., Frank B. Minirth, M.D. and Frank Wichern, Ph.D., in their book, *Introduction to Psychology and Counseling, Christian Perspectives and Applications,* agree that "character and behavior defects are correctable; physical defects seldom are. Therefore, parents who value and praise good character will help their children learn to behave properly while developing their feelings of self-worth that are vital to good mental health."

Many people carry hidden resentment toward God for not designing them the way they would have designed themselves. He did it this way because He wants to develop within each of us a Christ-like character so that we can experience life abundantly. It is foolish to think we are wiser than God. David wrote:

'For you created my inmost being; you knit me together in my mother's womb. I praise you because I am fearfully and wonderfully made; your works are wonderful, I know that full well. My frame was not hidden from you when I was made in the secret place. When I was woven together in the depths of the earth, your eyes saw my unformed body. All the days ordained for me were written in your book before one of them came to be.' Psalm 139:13-16.

"Through divine inspiration, although he knew nothing

about DNA and RNA, David knew that before we were born God designed us. While our bodies were being differentiated within our mothers' wombs, each 'inward part' was designed exactly as God intended—including both our strengths and weaknesses. We have the responsibility of living up to our potential, correcting any correctable defects. Our self-worth as well as our Christian witness will benefit from praising God for designing us the way we are."

The Building Blocks

We developed a simple, unique way to break down the complex subject of the *"inner man"* which you will find helpful; it is called *"The Building Blocks."*

The first building block for understanding human

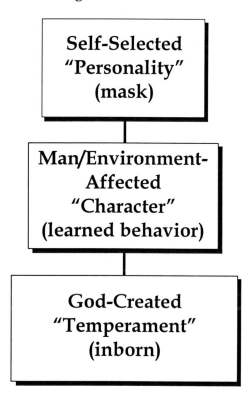

Self-Selected "Personality" (mask)

Man/Environment-Affected "Character" (learned behavior)

God-Created "Temperament" (inborn)

behavior is God-created. This is called our temperament. When we are conceived our unique temperament is placed within us by the order of God.

The second building block for understanding human behavior is that we are man/environment-affected. This is called our character. At birth, we begin interacting with our environment and our environment interacts with us. The environment is everything we see, hear, smell, feel and learn. These perceptions are forever locked into our brain, and they slightly mold and alter our temperament, thereby forming character (i.e., temperament x environment = character).

The third building block for understanding human behavior is that we are self-selected. This is called our personality, and is expressed in the way we perceive how we must behave to survive in the world in which we live. This may or may not be part of our temperament or character.

Temperament determines how much love and affection we need. For example, some babies are born with the need for very little stroking and holding. That need is placed within them by God. The character of others is formed in an environment where the parents hold and stroke them. These children will want to be stroked and held slightly more than their temperament shows. This increased need was placed within them by their parents, or, as we say, it is man/environment affected. This is called learned behavior. If, at somepoint in the child's life, he/she attempts to hold or stroke another person and is rejected, he/she will pull back and refrain from expressing love. The need to behave like this is self-selected and is called personality.

There is one major problem with personality. It is a mask we wear for the world and, as with any other mask, it cannot be worn for very long. Eventually, the person must revert back to temperament and character (for actions and reactions of behavior). This explains why a person acts differently at home than they do in public.

In order to understand others, we must gain insight

into the God-created part of their behavior which is their temperaments.

The understanding of temperament gives us a *special knowledge* of the inner workings of ourselves and others. It helps identify the pressures we, as humans, feel which are resulting from:

a. The world in which we live.
b. Our weaknesses or desires.

The understanding of temperament also helps us develop a stronger relationship with God by showing us how to let God work in our lives and how to interact with God in ways that are beneficial to us.

There are parts of man that are closely related and cannot be separated. Each is a determining factor in man's behavior; they are the physical, spiritual and emotional areas of mankind (mind, soul and body). Physical illness can affect our behavior as can spiritual darkness and emotional illness. Emotional illness; eating, sleeping and drinking habits; susceptibility to alcoholism, drug addiction and sexual abuse are determined in the temperament.

Temperament is a determining factor in:

a. Finding a career that is most comfortable for us.
b. Finding hobbies that will bring us the most satisfaction and enjoyment.
c. How we make decisions and take on responsibilities.
d. How dependent or independent we are.
e. Our spiritual development.

Happiness in marriage is greatly dependent on how well each spouse understands his or her partner's temperament and how willing he or she is to meet a partner's temperament needs.

Most temperament researchers and writers have the

simplistic view that an individual is one temperament, i.e., he is a Melancholy or she is a Choleric. This is seldom true. Humans are very complex individuals, physically, emotionally, and spiritually. For example, an individual may be a Melancholy in social interaction (Inclusion), a Sanguine in the decision-making area (Control) and a Phlegmatic in deeper relationships (Affection).

Biblical Background For
The Theory Of Temperament
❧ 2 ❧

The Theory of Temperament

"The spirit of man is the candle of the Lord, searching all the inward parts of the belly." Proverbs 20:27

The theory of temperament is a means for us to understand the inner workings of man (the temperament) and to shine like a light in a dark place.

Many authors and theologians have spent countless hours writing hundreds of books, theses and dissertations in an attempt to clarify the mystery concerning the inner man. This is a very complex subject, and anyone who attempts to explain it is usually accused of oversimplifying or over-complicating the subject; nevertheless, the mystery of man's soul and spirit is quite significant in the theory of temperament.

Two major schools of thought or theological doctrines concerning the inner man are the Dichotomists and the Trichotomists.

Dichotomists

Dichotomists believe there are only two essential elements in the constitution or makeup (the natural state of body or mind) of man:

a. The body — formed from the dust of the earth.
b. The soul — or principle of life. Genesis 2:7

They believe the soul to be the origin or source of the wholelife (whether that life is man or beast) and that it is the principle of all life: physical, intellectual, moral, religious. That is, there is not one substance, the soul, which feels and remembers and another substance, the spirit, that has conscience and the knowledge of God.

Dichotomists believe and teach that man is made up of two distinct parts: the body, which, of course, is the physical, and the soul, which includes the inner man in his entirety, i.e., will, emotions, intellect, etc. They believe that the spirit is simply the higher order or part of man's soul. The dividing factor between man and animal is that an animal has ONLY a lower soul, whereas man has both a lower soul and a higher soul.

"Who knoweth the spirit of man that goeth upward, and the spirit of the beast that goeth downward to the earth?" (Ecclesiastes 3:21)

Trichotomists

In support of their belief that man is a triune being, Trichotomists quote, *"The God of peace Himself sanctify you wholly; and may your spirit and soul and body be preserved entire, without blame unto the coming of the Lord."* (I Thessalonians 5:23) They believe there are three parts or essential elements of man.

God created man by enlivening lifeless matter that He formed into a body, and then creating a rational spirit and infusing it into the body (Genesis 2:7). At death the body returns to the dust of the earth from which it came and the spirit returns unto God who gave it (Ecclesiastes 12:7).

The soul of life, in the instance of the animal, is only the animal soul, which is physical and material in its nature, but perishes with the body in which it is the vital principle. However, the difference in the instance of man is that the soul is a higher principle, the rational soul, which was breathed by the Creator and made in His image.

There is, however, another school of thought that harmonizes with both the Dichotomist's and Trichotomist's interpretation of the natural and spiritual (I Corinthians 15:44). This school of thought refers to the redeemed (resurrected) body which will not be marked by the qualities of ordinary animal life (even if they are presently right and proper). The redeemed life will be opposed to everything carnal and is characterized by qualities that belong to the Spirit-led man. It refers to possession and control by the Holy Spirit as contrasted with the domination of the flesh (I Corinthians 3:1).

"For what man knoweth the things of man, save the spirit of man which is in him? Even so the things of God knoweth no man, but the Spirit of God." I Corinthians 2:11

"Now we have received, not the spirit of the world but the spirit which is of God; that we might know the things that are freely given to us of God." I Corinthians 2:12

"Which things also we speak, not in the words which man's wisdom teacheth, but which the Holy Ghost teacheth; comparing spiritual things with spiritual." I Corinthians 2:13

Thus, a spiritual body, when contrasted with a natural body, is a body free from fleshly lusts, and is elevated above the physical passions and appetites which are characteristic of the natural man. The spiritual body is in union with the Spirit of God and marked by the qualities which characterize the Spirit-led man.

"For the word of God is quick and powerful and sharper than any two-edged sword, piercing even to the dividing asunder of soul

and spirit and of the joints and marrow and is a discerner of the thoughts and intents of the heart." Hebrews 4:12

We all know that God is a Spirit. Man also is a spiritual being—created by God in His own image and likeness. God created man a spiritual being so He could communicate with him.

Adam communed (communicated) with God in the Garden of Eden in perfect fellowship and harmony. Adam's heart was totally satisfied as he experienced ultimate reality in fellowship with Him. Adam communed with God with his spirit. Adam's spirit had not yet fallen, because he was still in fellowship with God.

However, when Adam sinned he fell spiritually, and his spirit became estranged from God. Since that time, the human spirit, separated from God hungers and yearns to get back into fellow- ship with God— to that place that Adam once enjoyed. Did Adam sin and separate his heart from his spirit?

There is a spiritual hunger—a "heart hunger"— which supports this school of thought's belief that man is a triune being who wishes to be reconciled to God and to have fellowship with Him. Man does not always recognize that his heart cries out for fellowship with God. Therefore, that "heart hunger" sometimes drivesman into the things of the world in order to satisfy that "something" on the inside of him. Hunger for God will drive man, in his ignorance, to seek pleasure and material things—to meet his temperament needs in ungodly ways; it will drive him into obsessions and cults. The hunger that is on the inside of everyone has given birth to many of the religions of the world.

The reason a person becomes obsessed with those things is because his spirit is seeking, trying to find God. Man's spirit apart from God is never satisfied. That "heart hunger" will never be satisfied until a person accepts Jesus as his Savior and becomes a child of God.

Consider this: In man's endeavors to be reconciled to

God, he is, in fact, attempting to meet his temperament needs.

If an individual could meet every temperament need in ways that are pleasing to the Lord by drawing from the Spirit area, he would be perfect. This is, of course, idealistic. Man has not been able to reach the point where he can walk solely in the Spirit; sometimes he walks in the flesh.

Although temperament has not been specifically named, we believe there is ample proof that it does, in fact, exist. Temperament is made up of three specific areas:

a. Inclusion -The intellect.
b. Control -The will or will power.
c. Affection - The emotions.

Temperament is the part of man that determines how man interacts with his environment and how his environment interacts with him. Some researchers have stated their belief that the heart of man is his temperament. We believe that man is a triune being (created in God's image) made up of body, soul and spirit. Also we believe the temperament is found in the soul area.

The heart is found within the spirit and soul and is the linking devise between them. These different areas of the inner man are so closely related it is difficult to distinguish them, but within Biblical text they have different functions.

The spirit, created and given by God, is our source of life. See Psalm 104:29-30

As in John 6:63,"*It is the spirit that quickeneth; the flesh profiteth nothing: the words that I speak unto you, they are spirit, and they are life.*" When Jesus spoke these words, He linked our knowledge and understanding to His through the intellect of man.

"*But God hath revealed them unto us by His Spirit; for the Spirit searcheth all things, yea, the deep things of God.*"
(I Corinthians 2:10) What other way does God have to reveal things to man, and how else can He search and question except through the intellect of man?

"And Mary said, 'My soul doth magnify the Lord, and my spirit hath rejoiced in God my Savior'." (Luke 1:46-47) If we put these definitions into the preceding verses, then we can define these verses by using three areas of temperament. They might read as follows: "And Mary said, 'My will and my love of God show His greatness while my intellect finds happiness in the Lord my Savior'."

"Cast away from you all transgressions, whereby ye have transgressed; and make you a new heart and a new spirit: for why will ye die, O house of Israel?" (Ezekiel 18:31) Again, we see that two of the parts of man are identified for different reasons. The house of Israel must make a new spirit that is receptive to the Lord. The intellect, will, and emotions are renewed as part of the salvation experience.

From these previous verses we see a close relationship between spirit, soul, and heart. The soul includes the intellect (Inclusion), will (Control), and emotions (Affection). Temperament is made up of Inclusion, Control and Affection — intellect, will, and emotions.

By a simple process of logic, temperament is found in the soul area and might well be the linking devise between the two. If these contentions are true, the following is one of the most important statements of the theory of temperament: "Temperament is a determining factor in the spiritual development of man."

The Bible also refers to the fact that man's mind (Inclusion) and will (Control) interact with each other and cannot be separated. When a man is a nonbeliever, it is his will that prevents this intellectual process. This interaction is specifically shown in *"if anyone be willing to do (Greek) he shall know."* (John 7:17)

"For from within, out of the heart of men, proceed evil thoughts, adulteries, fornications, murders, thefts, covetousness, wickedness, deceit, lasciviousness, an evil eye, blasphemy, pride, foolishness: all these evil things come from within and defile the man." (Mark 7:21-23) From our intensive study of

temperament, we can identify which part of the temperament give rise to certain sins.

To explain further, evil thoughts and an evil eye are found in the Inclusion area of the temperament. Adulteries, fornication and lasciviousness (lusting) are found in the Affection area of the temperament. Sins of pride, foolishness and blasphemy are found in the Control area of the temperament. Wickedness, deceit, murder, thefts, and covetousness are a combination of two or more of the temperament needs of Inclusion, Control, and Affection.

Since we know that temperament defines how we perceive ourselves, the sin of pride comes from the temperament. Temperament is also made up of wants and needs. Therefore, sins like adultery and fornication are sinful ways the temperament has of meeting that person's need for love and affection. Temperament is also a contributing factor in what makes us angry and how deep the anger goes; sins of abusive anger are also found in the temperament.

Temperament is also made up of perfections we call strengths and, when properly used, bring glory to God.

"*Seeing ye have purified your soul in obeying the truth through the Spirit unto unfeigned love of the brethren, see that ye love one another with a pure heart fervently.*" (I Peter 1:22) In this verse we can see a clear picture of how temperament strengths can bring glory to God, for when a person loves with a pure heart, this love will be unconditional. Loving to this depth requires a balance in all three areas of the temperament—Inclusion, Control and Affection.

In order for our temperament perfections (strengths) to bring the greatest glory to God, we must first make up our minds to focus on the good and to overlook the bad. This is done with our intellectual energies (Inclusion). We must then decide to bend our will and, through that strength, meet the needs of another person. This takes an act of will (Control). To love unconditionally, our emotions must reach out and give love and affection to another person, regardless of our own wants and needs. This is in the Affection area of the temperament.

Temperament imperfections (weaknesses) determine the downfall of man. *"For as he thinketh in his heart, so is he: 'Eat and drink, saith he to thee;' but his heart is not with thee."* (Proverbs 23:7) This verse helps us understand that all three areas of a person's temperament must be "right with God."

The way a man perceives himself, his world and God will determine how he will behave. These perceptions are founded in the temperament. Therefore, on the basis of this premise, the temperament is the determining factor of who we are. However, our environment and our relationship with God determine who we will become.

"And the multitude of them that believed were of one heart and one soul: neither said any of them that ought of the things which he possessed was his own; but they had all things common." (Acts 4:32) And the multitude was of one heart. This reveals that all those present had the same perception as the apostles and were willing to interact with them.

"...That doeth the will of my Father in heaven" (Matthew 7:21) reinforces another contention of our temperament theory. We give up control of our lives and bend it to the Will of God. In other words, the Will of God must overcome our will (Control).

Another proof of the Biblical background for temperament is based on the writings of Dr. Tim LaHaye, who is one of the most published of Christian writers on the study of temperament. According to Dr. LaHaye, the Bible actually addresses itself to the temperaments and defines them when it speaks of the "generations."

"There is a generation that curseth their father, and doth not bless their mother. There is a gener-ation that are pure in their own eyes, and yet is not washed from their filthiness. There is a generation, O how lofty are their eyes! And their eyelids are lifted up. There is a generation, whose teeth are as swords, and their jaw teeth as knives, to devour the poor from off the earth, and the needy

among men." (Proverbs 30:11-14) These verses not only give us some background about the four different temperaments about which Dr. LaHaye does most of his writing but also pinpoint their most devastating weaknesses and how these weaknesses, when allowed to flourish, can and will destroy the spiritual man.

We must identify our temperament needs and pinpoint the ones that are currently causing us problems. In other words, our current problem is probably being caused by meeting a temperament need in an ungodly way. We must identify it and replace it with a godly method. Unmet needs become weaknesses.

"For the word of God is quick, and powerful, and sharper than any two-edged sword, piercing even to the dividing asunder of soul and spirit, and of the joints and marrow, and IS a discerner of the thoughts and intents of the heart." (Hebrews 4:12)

"And the very God of peace sanctify you wholly; and I pray God your whole spirit and soul and body be preserved blameless unto the coming of our Lord Jesus Christ." (I Thessalonians 5:23)

You are a spiritual being, you possess a soul and you live in a body.

Everyone knows it is possible to develop or educate your mind (your mind is part of your soul), and everyone also knows you can develop your body by exercise. Since it is true that you can develop your mind and your body, it must also be possible to develop your spirit. God would not give man the capacity for developing the mind and body without including man's spirit—or else man would not have been created a spiritual being.

Even the scientific/medical community recognizes this in terms of a therapeutic classification. According to Taber's Cyclopedic Medical Dictionary, F. A. Davis Company, Philadelphia, PA, 1968, "spiritual therapy is the application of spiritual knowledge in the treatment of all mental and physical disorders, based upon the assumption that MAN is a spiritual being living in a spiritual universe; that in proportion to his acceptance of this idea, and in proportion to his success in demonstrating it, he may control his body and the material elements in harmony with a Divine plan."

It is the spirit of man that contacts God. You do not contact God with your physical senses. It is the spiritual part of man that contacts God and experiences ultimate reality in fellowship with Him. Just like Adam in the Garden of Eden, it is through this communication that man's heart is totally satisfied. The only way man can find this reality (peace, love, joy, satisfaction) is through the rebirth of the human spirit by accepting Jesus as Savior.

"Therefore if any man be in Christ, he is a new creature: old things are passed away; behold, all things are become new." (II Corinthians 5:17)

A person cannot develop naturally without eating food. In the same way, a person cannot develop spiritually without feeding spiritually.

"It is written, Man shall not live by bread alone but by every word that proceedeth out of the mouth of God." (Matthew 4:4) The Word of God is spiritual food. The Word of God is to our spirits what natural food is to our bodies. If man does not eat and feed his body, he will starve to death. Also, man cannot grow (develop) spiritually by depriving the spirit of the Word of God.

It is the combination of all our research that has shown us:

Man is a physical, emotional and spiritual being with basic needs.
When man is seeking to meet these needs,
he is driven in his attempts to the things
of the world for his satisfaction.

Through identification of your individual needs (temperament needs) and teaching you "how to" meet these needs in godly ways—holy ways, we are teaching you to develop your spirit.

The following are the most important Biblical studies upon which we based temperament:

"Come unto me, all ye that labor and are heavy laden, and I will give you rest. Take my yoke upon you, and learn of me; for I am meek and lowly in heart: and ye shall find rest unto your souls. For my yoke is easy, and my burden is light." (Matthew 11: 28-30)

To understand how these verses played a part in the development of the theory of temperament, we must take each verse and put it into practical terms for today's life.

"Come unto me, all ye that labor and are heavy laden and I will give you rest." (verse 28) What does this mean to the individual? As Christians, we know that it does not mean that God will protect us from hard work, for in Genesis God ordained that man should live by the "sweat of his brow." Another translation of this verse could read, "Come to me, all you who are exhausted and weighed down beneath your burden."

To truly understand what this verse means, we must first understand what, in the human condition, causes a man to become exhausted spiritually, physically and emotionally.

Spiritually: A man becomes exhausted when he spends a lifetime searching for God and trying to earn His love by following a long line of meaningless religious laws and vain rituals. He becomes spiritually weary when all his efforts have been exhausted. Still he finds no peace in his soul, no joy in his life, and God is still a faraway and unattainable Being.

Physically: A man becomes exhausted when he, through his own neglect, pushes himself far beyond his physical endurance or when internal stress depletes his energy reserves.

Emotionally: A man becomes exhausted because exhaustion is the by-product of a person doing all the right things and abiding by all the rules, and yet internal stress leaves him without any means to withstand the stress of his environment.

Christ promised that we would receive rest from this

exhaustion, and how we receive this rest is found in Matthew 11: 29: *"Take my yoke upon you and learn of me."* The yoke that Christ speaks of in this verse is symbolic. In the life and times of Christ, His occupation was that of a carpenter. In those days the chief product of these craftsmen was not building homes but rather fitting and making yokes for the oxen.

Yokes were made so the owner could steer the beast, but this yoke was also made so the animal could work longer and more efficiently by tiring less under his heavy burdens. This mechanism was made of heavy wood, not padded as they are today. Therefore, they had to be measured and fitted perfectly. When two oxen were pulling a load, the yoke was designed for each animal to carry his share equally. When one animal was forced to do this very heavy work, the yoke equalized the load, allowing the animal to pull more with less effort.

Christ fitted these yokes perfectly for the animals, but in Matthew 11: 30 He tells us that He also fits the yoke perfectly for man. Christ knew that if the most empty-headed and stubborn of God's creations could benefit from a perfectly fitted yoke, then man, who is the most intelligent and gifted of God's creations, could benefit according to the gifts God has given him. The perfectly fitted yoke that Christ speaks about in these verses is the place that God has provided for each and every human that lives.

"For my yoke is easy..." is very important for us to understand. In this verse, the word "easy" does not mean

requiring little or no sacrifice. According to interpretation, the word Christ used was "Chrestas" which means well-fitting. Therefore, the proper translation is "For my yoke is well-fitting." What does well-fitting mean? According to our research, the placement of the individual into the Kingdom of God must fit all areas of his/her life. Christ calls the person into the right position as ordained by God and takes into account physical capabilities, spiritual maturity, and emotional makeup.

For example, it is doubtful that Christ would ever ask a 65-year-old man, suffering from a bad heart, to run a marathon to raise money for the needy, or ask a person who is a diabetic and must eat meals regularly to fast and pray for days. Either of these would cause physical breakdown, possibly death. It is also doubtful that Christ would put the infant Christians into a position where they would need to preach the Gospel into the far corners of the world, or ask the mature Christian who is well-versed and knowledgeable to sit in subservience to another where his wisdom and knowledge cannot be shared. This would cause spiritual breakdown and death to the soul.

The yoke of studying and reading long hours alone would probably not be given to an extrovert, nor would Christ place a dependent temperament in a situation where one must lead and make decisions for a worldwide ministry. These would cause a Christian to suffer emotional breakdown and even death. However, even though Christ has not called them to do these things, Christians may place themselves in this position and suffer these undesirable consequences.

Not only do these three things (spiritual, physical, emotional) come into play, Christ also takes into account our talents and intelligence. A person who cannot sing would do no good singing for the glory of God, nor would a person who could not write give glory by writing books. For the perfect glory of God to be given, these makeups must be perfect for the individual.

"Take my yoke upon you and learn of me." We have learned

that, for the Christian to reach and learn of Christ, he must have balance in his life. That can only be achieved if the person is in the position where God intends him to be. For example, if a person spends all his/her time on emotional pursuits, he/she has no energy left for the spiritual side. If they develop physically, they are denying the other parts and will suffer imbalance in those areas. If a person spends all his/her time in spiritual pursuits, the physical and emotional sides suffer. The stress caused by this imbalance will prevent him/her from practicing what he/she learned in his/her spiritual pursuits.

This balance must go one step further. There must be complete balance in the inner man. The soul and spirit must be in balance or the Christian cannot grow. If the heart is the binding and balancing agent between the soul and the spirit, then there must be complete balance among Inclusion, Control and Affection to keep the soul and spirit in balance. Since the soul is the intermediate between body and spirit, if the soul is out of balance, the body and spirit will also be out of balance.

When we accept the perfectly fitting yoke that Christ has provided for us, rest, peace, and joy are the results. Then we are able to learn of Christ. His words and His ways free us from the stress and pressures that plague all of us. The external man can work more efficiently and do more, both for himself and for the Kingdom of God. When we accept the perfectly fitting yoke that Christ has provided for us, the inner man finds balance and is provided with love, joy, and peace.

When people are physically sick or exhausted, or emotionally stressed or strained, they are short-tempered, depressed, withdrawn and not pleasant to other people. They may even be angry and question the methods and motives of God. In this state, they are hard to reach for Christ. They lack the strength to do the good works that God has given them to do, and they lack the strength or willpower to withstand the persecution of Satan.

The person who is suffering from emotional exhaustion

begins to suffer physical problems such as fatigue, high blood pressure, stomach disorders and susceptibility to infectious diseases.

When any one of these things happens, God, Christ, and the fruit of this relationship seem far away and unattainable. Because of any of the above problems, the spiritual part of man turns his back on God and begins to worship power, money, position, or other people. The emotional side suffers, for, no matter how hard they try, they cannot fill the void that is within. In turn, the physical man begins to suffer and break down. Not only does the man suffer, but his ability to witness for God is weakened. How can the individual speak of love, joy, and peace when there is none in his life? How can the person tell of forgiveness when he has no forgiveness? How can he witness for the greatness of Christ when his life does not show that greatness?

This is the chain reaction that occurs when the yoke (place) that man has put himself into is not the place that God has designed. To learn of God, we must accept the yoke which He has designed for us in order to bring balance into our lives.

"...For I am meek and lowly in heart." This part of the verse gives us some very important information about Christ. Throughout the New Testament Christ tells us that He came to serve, and we all know this. He gave the ultimate in service by dying on the cross and being resurrected bodily from the grave for the forgiveness of our sins. There are so many other ways that Christ was of service to mankind. These words tell us that Christ had the heart of a servant.

He served man (by presenting God's truth), and freed him from the harsh and almost impossible Jewish laws. He freed people from demons and spirits. He also healed the sick and cured the afflicted. He fed the thousands and loved the unlovable. Not only did these acts bring glory to God, but they were also of service to the emotional, physical, and spiritual part of man. "...For I am meek and lowly in heart" means that He had the heart of a servant and was the perfect servant. What does the perfect servant do? He serves and provides for all the needs of the person or people he serves. Christ is the perfect servant; thus, He can provide for all of our needs.

Physically: Information is provided to help us understand what is necessary to establish and maintain the best possible health for our bodies. Spiritually: He provides us with the relationship with the Omnipotent Being that will give order and meaning to our lives and immortality. Emotionally: Christ provides us with Inclusion (surface relationship and socialization), Control (power and control), and Affection (deep, fulfilling personal relationships, love, and affection).

In practical application, this verse gives us all the information needed to apply the theory of temperament. When this is reinforced by the life and times of Christ, it gives us the understanding of the thrust of this theory. Simply put, the theory of temperament is helping to find the yoke (our place) that God has designed for us. This place (or His plan/calling on our life) can be identified, for the most part, by the temperament. Not only does Christ allow us to have the information that helps place us in the perfect environment God has designed for us, He can also provide for any of our temperament needs that are not being met, thus allowing us to achieve perfect balance in the inner man.

Think of the Kingdom of God as a jigsaw puzzle. For the picture to be complete, each piece is fitted and placed in the exact spot where it is needed. This is true with the individual. Each person is tailor-made for a certain position, and only when each piece is properly placed will the total picture be revealed. If a person chooses not to go into that place designed for them, they will forever feel as if they do not belong and are outside of the finished product. Only when they are positioned in that final place will they be happy, fulfilled and part of the total picture that God has designed for them. (This is man surrendering his will to God's will.)

Think of the inner man as a scale. In order to provide for all areas of the inner man, perfect balance must be maintained.

By learning who we are according to the laws of creation, we are free to be the way God created us to be. Thus, we are finding peace in our circumstances and the place God has designed for us.

Man is a spiritual being created by God with a precise order and balance of body, soul and spirit. Not only was man created with this perfect order and balance, but God has also designed a place for each person in the schemata of His creation. It is the blending, binding, and balancing of the body, soul, and spirit that enables man to accept the position God has for him.

For man to realize (find) his place in the scheme of the universe and God's creation, he must understand his temperament.

The temperament is made up of three specific areas: Inclusion, Control and Affection. Temperament has not previously been identified as a part of the precise order of man. Temperament is the missing link in this balance.

The heart is the binding, balancing, and blending agent that overlaps the soul and the spirit and provides order within man.

The temperament areas: Inclusion, Control and Affection are found in the soul area. If the soul and spirit are to remain in balance, then the three areas of the temperament Inclusion, Control and Affection must also be balanced. If the soul and spirit are out of balance, the physical man will break down. If we know this order, then we can help provide a means to achieve balance.

The theory of temperament is, in part, a means by

which man is given the understanding of his temperament and the knowledge to find balance and the perfect place God has designed for him.

With this knowledge we have the ability to find balance between body, soul, and spirit, and to be the best that God created us to be.

It is important to understand that temperament is inborn and placed in us when God breathes into us, the breath of life. Also, temperament does not change. Some people think that when the Lord saves people, He changes their temperaments. He does not change the color of their eyes and He does not change their temperaments. However, the person's temperament strengths begin to be used for the glory of the Lord, rather than the glory of self. In addition, the individual's temperament weaknesses become subject to the Lord and He turns them into strengths.

Historical And Scientific Background

❧ 3 ❧

The purpose of this chapter is to demonstrate that historically the scientific community has studied temperament and has advanced theories regarding their studies which are varied but similar. The information given here is not an exhaustive study of temperament history, but does provide a concise overview of fundamental information.

Another purpose of this chapter is to demonstrate that, even though the secular community has a foundation for the theory of temperament, they have neglected to use this information. This study takes the view that this has happened because the secular community has refused to recognize that man was created, not evolved. The theory of temperament presupposes a creationist view of life.

Any study of the temperaments must go back 2,400 years to the early Greek historian, Hippocrates. According to Dr. Tim LaHaye, the study of temperaments may go back even further, to Solomon, the writer of the book of Proverbs.

Hippocrates (460-370 B.C.)

Hippocrates was the first to bring to light the theory of temperament, even though he may have been building on the thoughts of Impedocles (495435 B.C.). Since Hippocrates did not have the scientific tools that are available today, his theories were based upon his observations of man's behavior. According to Hippocrates, man's behavior was governed by the color of bile within a person's body. These body fluids, which he called humors, were divided into four classifications: blood (Sanguine), black bile (Melancholy), yellow bile (Choleric), and phlegm (Phlegmatic). He believed that an excess of these fluids would cause the person to behave according to that fluid, i.e., a person who had an overabundance of black bile would be an extremely dark, moody person, as in the Melancholy. As we know today, the theory of humors has proven to be scientifically unsound, but his theories have given us some basic understanding of the differences in human behavior.

Galen (131-200)

Galen developed the first typology of temperament, which he presented in his well-known dissertation "De Temperamentis." Galen searched for physiological reasons for the differences in behavior of the human. Galen's theories have been partially proven in psychopharmacological and endocrinological research.

Maimonides (1135-1204)

Maimonides was a rabbi, physician and philosopher who attempted to codify the Jewish oral law in his writing of the Mishna Torah while also writing volumes on religion and philosophy. According to Maimonides, humors (temperament) are responsible for the differences between the speed of learning, ease of understanding, and excellence of memory, and the differences between courageous versus craven attitudes.

Nicholas Culpeper (1616-1654)

The four major temperaments as described by Hippocrates remained virtually unchanged until the seventeenth century with the writings of Nicholas Culpeper. Culpeper disregarded the idea of "humors" or "fluids" to define human behavior, yet held to the theory of temperament to identify human behavior. He felt that people were not one temperament but were affected by two temperaments— dominant and recessive.

Immanuel Kant (1724-1804)

Kant was a German philosopher who was regarded as "a formidable intellectual giant" of his time. Anthropology has been interpreted as "...Kant's entire philosophical system." According to Kant, temperaments are caused by the vital power of the blood and the temperature of the blood. Kant made two divisions and gauged the degree of feelings according to the temperature of the blood. The Sanguine is light-blooded and the Melancholy is heavy-blooded. The Choleric and its opposite, the Phlegmatic, have cold blood. On the basis of this philosophical observation, a person can be of only one temperament and if two temperaments associate with one another they will neutralize each other. On this basis, there can be no blending, i.e., Sanguine-Choleric.

Alfred Adler (1879-1937)

In 1927 Adler interpreted Hippocrates' four temperaments, the Sanguine, Choleric, Melancholic and Phlegmatic.

Historically, we believe that Alfred Adler was the first to give us functioning of the temperaments. Adler believed that the Sanguine was the healthiest type because they were not subject to severe deprivations and humiliation, had very few feelings of inferiority, and strived for superiority in a happy, friendly manner. The Choleric was the very aggressive and intense temperament, always striving to be on top and willing to expend great amounts of energy to get there. The Melancholy felt inferior and lacked initiative in overcoming most obstacles. The Melancholy was the worrier and lacked the self-discipline to make decisions when risks were involved. The Melancholy was not antisocial, but chose not to associate. The Phlegmatic was the person who had lost contact with life and was not impressed by, or with, anything in it. He was also described as depressed, slow and sluggish. In 1935 Adler developed his own typology, but he did not believe that typology either. He believed that classification was an unfruitful means of dealing with humans and was only useful in helping other people to learn of temperaments.

Ivan Pavlov (1849-1936)

Pavlov was one of the most famous of Russian psychologists, best known for his typology of conditioning in his experiments with dogs. In addition to these experiments, Pavlov observed mental patients for years. Because of the differences in the excitatory and inhibitory responses of these patients, he divided these people into the same four types as Hippocrates—the Choleric, the Melancholy, the Sanguine and the Phlegmatic. The Choleric and Melancholy were the two extreme types. The Sanguine and the Phlegmatic were the two equalizing types.

Hans J. Eysenck (1916- 1997)

Hans J. Eysenck is a modern contributor to the theory of temperament and a well-known German psychologist who received training at the University of London. In his research he sought to analyze personality differences using a psycho-statistical method. Eysenck's research led him to believe that temperament is biologically based.

Tim LaHaye (1926-)

Dr. LaHaye is a well-known author, educator, minister and counselor. He is the founder and president of Family Life Seminars, the American Coalition for Traditional Values, and the founder and past-president of Christian Heritage College. Dr. LaHaye has authored at least twenty-three books, of which at least four deal with the topic of temperament and its relationship to human behavior. Although Dr. LaHaye's books are not written in scientific format, they are important. His writings and research confirm that there are other Christian professionals who believe that understanding temperament is imperative in the understanding of man.

The preceding information is brief, spans 2,400 years, and represents only a minute percentage of the historical background for the study of temperament. However, we believe it is sufficient to show the reader that there is, indeed, a strong scientific and historical base for the theory of temperament.

Drs. Richard and Phyllis Arno

Review Of The Literature

◈ 4 ◈

The intention of this chapter is to provide information from experimental psychologists, who are basically nomothetic, to build a foundation for genetically based behavior. This study will not be in-depth, but the overview will be sufficient for this purpose.

The nomothetic researchers point us to the fact that the personality traits are inferred from consistencies in speech and behavior. It is also pointed out by the nomothetic psychologists that traits which are common can be measured. Emotional instability or anxiety and introversion and extroversion can be psychometrically measured. The five psychologists we will present are: Hans J. Eysenck, J. Shields, Jeffrey Gray, Arnold H. Buss, and Robert Plowman.

According to Eysenck, there is some important information we need in order to understand temperament. Two
of his most important tenets for this study are as follows:

1. Different personality traits of people are
   determined by heredity.

2. Different personality traits can be
   measured by a questionnaire.

Jeffrey Gray of the University of Oxford critiqued Dr.
Eysenck's theory, adding much more interesting information
and many points to the theory of temperament. Dr. Gray
proposes that susceptibility to punishment and reward are
in direct correlation to the traits of extroversion, introversion,
and neuroticism. The dimensions of anxiety and impulsivity
correlate with the rates of susceptibility to punishment and
reward respectively.

In 1962 J. Shields conducted intensive studies on
monozygotic (identical) twins. He administered a series of
tests and produced some very important findings that are
beneficial to our studies. According to Shields, monozygotic
twins not only share a likeness in physical attributes but also
share behavioral and personality traits. This was verified in
his studies of monozygotic twins who were raised separately.
Even in their different environments, they tended to be
amazingly similar in behavior and personality. This study
also showed that monozygotic twins, brought up separately,
are much more alike than dizygotic (fraternal) twins brought
up together. This is very important to us, for it indicates that,
because of the shared genetic coding of the identical twins,
the physical and behavioral traits of these twins are both
determined by heredity. The fraternal twins do not have

this same coding but share a different genetic background, so not only are their physical traits different but also their temperaments.

In their book, A Temperament Theory of Personality Development, Arnold H. Buss and Robert Plowman deal with the genetic factors of temperament. According to their writing, the most important factor in the development of man's behavior is heredity. This factor distinguishes temperament from the other aspects of human personality. According to their studies, children start life with genetically different traits that account for their behavior, and these stay with the person throughout life and are only modified by the environment.

Buss and Plowman use different names for the aspects of the temperament. They are the following:

a. Activity
b. Emotionality
c. Sociability
d. Impulsivity

These we found in definition to be extremely close to those developed by Will Schutz in his FIROB. They were modified and expanded by the authors of this book and they are as follows:

a. Inclusion
b. Control
c. Affection

These are only a few scientific writings available to us in the study of temperament. There are many other study sources from which we have taken information, including the following:

*The First Warsaw Conference, Temperament and
Personality, 1974.*
Pavlov and Beyond, Jan Strelau.
*The Second Warsaw Conference, Temperament,
Need for Stimulation and Activity, 1979.*
*The American Psychological Association, Graduate Study
in Psychology, Washington, D.C., 1986.*

This literature reinforces our own research that the temperament of a person is determined on the day of conception and will continue throughout the individual's life. Also, temperament is the determining factor of how we interact with our environment and how our environment interacts with us.

Creationists Versus Evolutionists

⚬ 5 ⚬

In the Christian community, we know that the universe and all the laws that govern it are by the direct order of God. All of man's intricacies and the rules governing them are by the order of God. In Christian psychology we understand that there is a better knowledge outside of ourselves and there are rules that are as perfect as our governor, God.

Man is a direct, "hands on" creation of God. We also know that each birth in this world is by direct ordinance of God. Because each person is a unique creation of God, we have no right to question that creation. As Christians following the Bible, we have standards by which to judge the behavior of man and a blueprint to follow to effect change. Because we know that the temperament is given to a person at birth by God, we believe that we can use an understanding of temperament to help ourselves and others. (Psalm 139: 13-16)

The most popular theories used in psychology today were developed by Albert Ellis, Frederick Perls, Carl Rogers, and Sigmund Freud. These theories are based on humanismand, therefore, evolutionary thinking. The followers of these theories have made little progress with their knowledge and ability to help people. They believe they are an authority unto themselves, and they follow only the human knowledge at their disposal. They have closed their minds to the fact that there is a higher being, God, who interacts with each of us separately and with mankind as a whole. Their biological assumption is that the genetic base for each person is determined like a roll of the dice; certain things are put in and certain things come out randomly.

This theory provides evolutionists with another wrong premise: man's life on earth is at random, like a lottery, as is his behavior. They have no standard by which to judge the behavior of man; thus, they have no basis upon which to effect change.

The religion of humanism has indoctrinated our society to the point that even Christians find humanistic thoughts filtering into their minds. We may find ourselves believing that their theories are law, but in reality they have taken the laws of the universe and twisted them to support their religion. Humanists cite numerous laws of the universe which are true, yet the basic premises of evolution can be disproved by the very laws they cite. For example, they cannot tell us when evolution started or where it will end. Therefore, humanists must assume that man will eventually evolve into a higher creature. Can the lower creature at sometime in the future be man? These are questions asked by the Christian, yet the humanists can give us no answer. Even the theory of evolution cannot explain how the laws of the universe evolved or where they came from.

In actuality, the Christian belief of man and his creation

is more provable by the same laws cited by the humanists. In fact, the scientific observations that have been made to date confirm the creationist's model. The basic laws of the universe, i.e., the law of gravity, the law of energy and matter, and the laws of thermodynamics, function the same now as they have in the past and support a creationist view.

The most basic and accepted law of the universe recognized and used in all fields of science supports a belief in an omnipotent God. This law relates to an effect and its cause—no effect is quantitatively "greater" nor qualitatively "superior" to its cause. An effect can be lower than its cause but never higher. From this law the creationists have reasoned:

The First Cause of limitless space—must be infinite.

The First Cause of boundless energy—must be omnipotent.

The First Cause of endless time—must be eternal.

The First Cause of universal interrelationship—must be omnipresent.

The First Cause of infinite complexity—must be omniscient.

The First Cause of moral values—must be moral.

The First Cause of spiritual values—must be spiritual.

The First Cause of human responsibility—must be volitional.

The First Cause of human love—must be loving.

The First Cause of life—must be living.

Since the universe has limitless space, endless time, boundless energy, and universal interrelationships, the cause must be greater. Since man's being is a moral, spiritual, loving, living being with infinite complexities, the cause must be greater. Infinite, eternal, omnipotent, omnipresent, omniscient, moral, spiritual, volitional, loving, and living can describe no other cause than God.

For the evolution precess to begin, complex molecules must be formed by cosmic radiation. Moreover, those complex molecules must undergo billions of mutations to eventually yield a "lifeform." This idea itself violates the Second Law of Thermodynamics which states: The total disorder of a system increases as a result of any natural process. The odds that such a succession of events could actually occur are beyond comprehension.

In order to give you a better understanding of these odds, consider this. A person sets a keg of dynamite inside a printing company and blows it up. All of the debris is catapulted up into the air. While in the air, the debris collects itself together and forms an unabridged Webster's dictionary and falls back to earth. Upon examination of this magnificently collected debris that fell from the sky, one observes that the dictionary not only created itself, it was hand autographed by Noah Webster.

From even the limited information presented here, one can see that it takes more faith to believe in evolution than in creation. Evolution is a religion because it requires faith to believe it.

Why Temperament Is So Important

❧ 6 ❧

Thus far, we have looked at the biblical, historical, and scientific backgrounds of temperament. We have also seen how humanists, who have had this knowledge much longer than the Christian community, have been unable to use this information for the betterment of man.

Since the fall of Adam, man has been an imperfect being. His physical being ages, becomes sick, dies, and decays. The emotional man commits sins, brings forth evil, is self-satisfying, and breaks under enough stress. The spiritual man at times turns his back on God or denies His existence. This is all part of the imperfection of man.

The temperament also has imperfections (or weaknesses), manifested by the free choice to accept or reject, and perfections, which are defined as strengths. As in the spiritual man, the emotional side of man also has a free choice of will. We can rise to our strengths and use them to glorify God, or we can sink to the weaknesses and use them to separate us from God. However, this choice of free will is removed from us if we are not made aware of our strengths and weaknesses.

For example, in one specific temperament the weakness is extremely low self-esteem. Because of this low self-esteem, the person is continually searching his environment for confirmations of his low self-perception. This is a definite temperament weakness, and the person is unaware that he is sinking to this weakness. He really believes the world does not like him and is rejecting him. He can point to innumerable occasions to prove his point. Since the world with its evils cannot like this man, then how can God, with His goodness, accept him?

To this person, God has turned His back on him. But in actuality, he has been sinking into the temperament weakness which has caused him to separate himself from God. Thus, "man turns his back on God—not God turning His back on man."

The free choice of will has been removed because this person does not know or understand this as a weakness. Once we identify our temperament, know and understand our weaknesses, we can learn to rise above this weakness and develop our relationship with God.

We must come to the point when we realize that these weaknesses are not really weaknesses at all. They are the result of our response to our unmet temperament needs, and trying to meet those needs in ungodly ways, while trying to get back into communion with God.

The temperament is extremely important for another reason—it makes a person unique. For example, certain persons cannot feel loved unless they are told so every day. They love being constantly touched, held, and stroked. To them, hugging, kissing, and touching are all very important. Other persons may not need to be told in words but must be shown in actions. Their friends and family must be truthful, reliable and dependable. If they are hugged and kissed or touched too much, they feel their space is being violated. If you are not aware of these differences, then there is no way you can develop and maintain healthy relationships.

Some individuals ask, "What did I do to make my child so shy and backward?" or "What is wrong with me? I have a beautiful home and a great family, but I love going out and being with people." The answer to both of these questions is, "Nothing." A parent can have an effect on children, but their effect is not as great as the effect of temperament. A shy person was simply created by God to be shy. And there is nothing wrong with a person who loves to go out and be with people. This person was also created by God to be exactly the way he/she is.

An oak tree is an oak tree, and an apple tree is an apple tree. We do not criticize the oak because it is not an apple, or the apple because it is not an oak. We only see the beauty of the two different creations of God and accept their individual places in the scheme of creation. So should it be with people. We must not criticize them for what they are and try to make them into something different. We must love them the way God created them to be and we must love and accept ourselves as God has created us to be.

OAK TREE   APPLE TREE

Drs. Richard and Phyllis Arno

Interpersonal Situations

❧ 7 ❧

People need people! This is a law of human nature that is inescapable. People of all temperament types need other people in order to be totally fulfilled and mentally healthy. From a Sanguine to a Melancholy, from extrovert to introvert, people cannot be fulfilled emotionally without other people. Even spiritually, people need other people because God put that need into them. We all need people:

    a. For conversation.
    b. For association.
    c. For encouragement.
    d. To give and receive love, affection, recognition, and approval.

Interpersonal situations are when people associate, spend time, encourage, talk to and/or give love, affection, recognition, and approval.

In the area of interpersonal relationships, the difference between the temperament types is in the degree of need each person has for other people. That is, an extrovert displays a high social need while an introvert displays a low social need. These degrees of need are measured in two terms:

1. Expressed needs
2. Responsive (wanted) needs

The expressed and responsive needs are associated in three basic action and reaction areas:

1. Inclusion (social)
2. Control (decision-making)
3. Affection (deeper relationships)

These needs are placed within man by God and are similar to biological needs. A biological need is defined as a physical need that is required to maintain the physical man. The non-realization of a biological need will cause undesirable consequences such as physical breakdown or death.

Temperament needs are placed within the emotional man and are defined as emotional needs that are required to maintain the emotional man. The non-realization of a temperament need will cause undesirable consequences such as emotional breakdown or death.

The basic physical needs are:

1. Food.
2. Water.
3. Oxygen.
4. Rest.

The emotional needs (temperament needs) are to:

1. Associate with other people.
2. Control and take power.
3. Be controlled.
4. Give love and affection.
5. Receive love and affection.

We identify these needs within the temperament as Inclusion, Control, and Affection.

An interpersonal situation involves two or more people who consider each other for a purpose. That purpose, or course of action, we shall call decision D. D is described from the point of view of one of the participants or an outside observer. Also, decision D is specified during a stated time interval. Thus, the complete statement of an interpersonal situation is:

From the standpoint of observer O (or A or B), A encounters B for decision D during time interval T1 to Tn. One criterion for A's choice is his expectation of B's response to his choice.

When one person is interacting with another, they are doing so for a reason. That reason can be for social involvement, to take control of them, to show them love and affection, or for other reasons.

During the interaction, if A makes a move or chooses a course of action, he will choose the one that he believes will get the desired reaction from B. One of the determining factors for A's behavior is how A believes B will react to his behavior.

Example:

If one person wants love and affection from another person, then the course of action (behavior) that the person undertakes will be determined by what he believes he needs to do in order to receive love and affection from the desired person at that time.

Another criterion used in the determination of decision D (course of action) is the physical presence of the second person. That is, if they are seeking love and affection from one who is presently with them, it would be different than if the other person were not presently with them.

Example:

Holding hands versus writing a love letter.

An interpersonal relationship can be one person interacting with one person, or one person interacting with a group of people. When someone deals with a group of people in an interpersonal relationship, that group of people is combined to be one entity.

Example:

A pastor of a church can interact one-to one with his parishioners as individuals or, when he stands in his pulpit, he combines the number of those individuals into a group and interacts with it as one person. He is preaching to the congregation or he is teaching the Body of Christ, and in this situation the interaction is as one entity.

There is another interpersonal relationship that man needs to establish and develop. This relationship is the relationship between God and man. God interacts with man as an individual, one-to one, or to mankind as a group. In either case, all of God's interaction with man is on the interpersonal level.

God created man for fellowship with Him. It has been said that there is a "God-shaped" void in each one of us that causes us to need a relationship with Him. Since man is created in God's image, and we know God wants to fellowship (interact) with man, then we conclude that man's need for

God and for others has been placed in him by God.

On the emotional level, man suffers when the need for a relationship with God is not met, just as the emotional man suffers when his need for other people is not met. Of course, there are much greater spiritual consequences when man's need for God is not met.

Example:

A (man) takes account of B (God) for decision D. Or the criterion for A's (man's) decision D is A's (man's) perception of B's (God's) reaction to that decision D.

A simple example is when man is physically sick and wants to be healed by God. Man will undertake the behavior which he perceives will get the needed response (healing).

The second criterion for the course of action is physical presence. If this person perceives God to be a close person whom he can touch, then he will undertake a behavior that is different than if he believes God is a faraway Being who cannot be touched.

Even the act of asking for redemption is an interpersonal relationship. A (man) wants salvation.

A (man) takes account of B (Jesus Christ) for decision D (salvation). One criterion for A's (man's) course of action (behavior) is what he believes he must do to receive salvation. One criterion he uses in the determination is his perception of Christ's reaction to his behavior.

This is part of the reason why people within the same religious and denominational backgrounds will interact differently with God.

The spiritual man and the emotional man are directly linked when it comes to establishing and maintaining a deep relationship with God. For man to reach spiritual maturity, the emotional part of man interacts with God to meet emotional needs—thus creating a stronger spiritual bond.

When a person is involved in an interpersonal relationship with man or God, he/she will sometimes undertake behaviors they know will elicit an undesired response from the other person.

When man engages in these behaviors, he will separate himself from that relationship to avoid the undesirable consequences of his behavior. When he undertakes a behavior that he perceives is displeasing to God, he will separate himself from God to avoid the consequences of his behavior; thus, the emotional part of man causes the spiritual part of man to suffer.

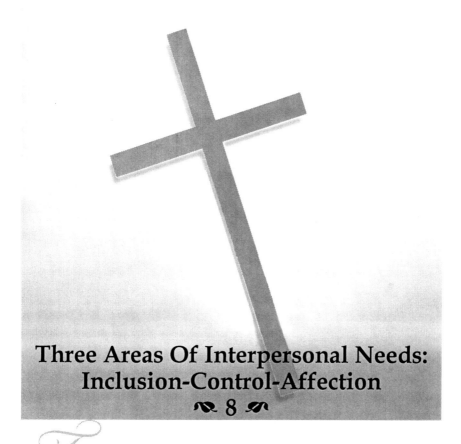

Three Areas Of Interpersonal Needs: Inclusion-Control-Affection
✎ 8 ✎

These three areas govern our behavior in interpersonal relationships and also determine how we approach the rest of our lives. The areas of Inclusion, Control, and Affection are distinguishable and measurable, yet they are interwoven throughout the behavior of man. These needs also reinforce our knowledge of creation and the omnipotence of God. Only the "hands on" creation of an omnipotent Being allows for such differences and order within the behavior of man.

In a "nutshell," Inclusion determines who is in or out of the relationship; Control determines who maintains the power and makes decisions for the relationship; and Affection determines how emotionally close or distant the relationship.

49

Inclusion

Inclusion is the need to establish and maintain a satisfactory relationship with people in the area of surface relationships, association, and socialization. The relationships include parties, social gatherings, and people who come in and out of our lives every day. The need within the temperament ranges from approaching a good many people for association (socializing, surface relationships) to approaching only a select few.

The second need in Inclusion is wanting people to approach us for association and socializing. This need is measured from a scale of wanting almost everyone to approach us for association to wanting almost no one to approach us for association.

Some terms we use to describe this association are: interact, mingle, belong, communicate, companion, attend, member, togetherness, join, extrovert, introvert, exclusion, isolate, outcast, outsider, lonely, detached, withdrawn, abandoned, and ignored. Inclusion is unlike the temperament need of Affection in that it does not involve the strong emotional attachments to another person.

Inclusion Need #1 is the need to establish and

maintain satisfactory surface relationships (association and socialization).

Inclusion Need #2 is our desire for wanting people to approach us for association and socialization.

Inclusion is unlike the temperament need of Control in that Inclusion concerns itself with the prominence of the social encounter. Control concerns itself with determining which of the participants in the interpersonal situation is dominant.

The need that a person is attempting to meet in the area of Inclusion is the perception of feeling significant or worthwhile.

Control

Control is the need to establish and maintain a satisfactory relationship with people in regard to control and power. This need will determine who needs to maintain control and hold the power in the interpersonal situation. The need for control within the temperament ranges from maintaining control over everyone's behavior to maintaining control over no one's behavior. The second area of need within the temperament is measured in wanting no one to control our behavior to wanting everyone to take control of our behavior.

Control is the decision-making process between people, and is described in such terms as power, authority, dominance, influence, control, ruler, superior, officer, leader, rebellion, resistance, follower, anarchy, submission, and henpecked.

Control Need #1 is the need to establish and maintain a satisfactory relationship with people in regard to control and power.

Control Need #2 is the need within the temperament measured by wanting no one to control our behavior to wanting everyone to take control over our behavior.

Control differs from Inclusion because Control is the need for dominance within the interpersonal situation, not prominence of the relationship, i.e., the power behind the throne.

Control is different from Affection because it has to do with the need for power in the relationship rather than emotional closeness.

The perception of feeling competent is the need the person is attempting to meet in the area of Control.

Affection

Affection is the need to establish and maintain a satisfactory relationship with others in areas of love and affection. The needs within the temperament range from showing love and affection to a great many people to showing love and affection to only a select few.

The second area of need within the temperament ranges from wanting love and affection from everyone to wanting love and affection from no one.

Affection is unique within the temperament because it can only occur person to person. In the areas of Inclusion and Control a group of people can be combined to be associated with or controlled as one, but in the area of Affection, the relationship can only be one person to one person. The intimacy of the temperament need can only be achieved by the close, personal, emotional feeling between two people. To become emotionally close to someone, there is an element of confiding innermost desires, anxieties, and feelings. A strong emotional tie is usually accomplished by a unique relationship regarding the sharing of these feelings.

Affection Need #1 is the need to establish and maintain a relationship with others in areas of love and affection.

Affection Need #2 is the need within the temperament which is measured by whether one wants love and affection from everyone he meets or from very few.

The feeling that one's self is lovable is the need we attempt to meet in the area of Affection.

Temperament Needs in Interpersonal Relationships. These three parts of temperament needs have unique functions in interpersonal relationships. As we apply these needs to the interpersonal relationship statement, you will recognize how they affect man's behavior.

Interpersonal Relationship Statement:

A takes account of B for decision D. One criterion for A's decisionis A's perception ofhow B will react to that decision.

Inclusion Example:

A considers B for his temperament need for association. A would like to associate with B and must plan actions that will assure that B will accept interaction. Thus, A's behavior is determined by whatever action will receive the desired response to get B to associate.

A needs to be approached for association by B. A will take a plan of action or behave in a way that A believes will guarantee that B will approach A for association.

Control Example:

A considers B for the purpose of controlling B. The plan of action A will take is determined by what A believes must be done to control the behavior of B.

A needs to have A's behavior controlled by B. A will undertake the behavior A believes necessary for B to control A.

Affection Example:

A will take account of B for the purpose of showing love and affection. A will undertake a behavior which A believes will let B know that A is being loving and affectionate.

A considers B for the purpose of obtaining love and

affection. A will undertake a behavior that A believes will obtain love and affection from B.

The interpersonal relationship will be established and maintained according to the temperament needs that the individual is endeavoring to meet. This illustrates how temperament needs determine how we behave.

Inclusion, Control, and Affection are not only needs within the temperament that must be met, but are also determining factors in other personality traits. The area of Inclusion determines intellectual energies, whether we relate better to tasks or people, and how impulsive our behavior may be. The area of Control determines how well we make decisions, carry out responsibilities, and how dependent or independent we are. The area of Control also determines how strong our will is. The area of Affection will determine how many of our emotions we share, or how emotionally guarded, or open we are. This area also helps determine the depth of our feelings. This area of temperament determines how intimate we are with the deep relationships in our life.

The temperament need of Inclusion concerns itself with whether or not a relationship exists and the behaviors involved that will establish and maintain a surface relationship, or the behaviors involved to disassociate from the surface relationships.

Inclusion determines:

Who is in or out of the relationship.

Control determines:

Who maintains the power and makes decisions for the relationship.

Affection determines:

How emotionally close or far the relationship.

Inclusion, Control, and Affection are not only needs within the temperament that must be met but are also determining factors in other personality traits.

Inclusion determines:

Social interaction — whether we relate better to tasks or to people, and the impulsiveness of the behavior.

Control determines:

How well we make decisions, how well we carry out responsibilities, and how dependent or independent we are. The area of Control also determines how strong our will is.

Affection determines:

How many of our emotions we share, how emotionally guarded or emotionally open we are. This area also determines how intimate we are with the extremely close people in our lives, and it also determines the depth of our feelings.

These needs also reinforce our knowledge of creation and the omnipotence of God. It is the "hands on" creation of an omnipotent Being that allows for such differences and yet such order, all within the behavior of man.

All good works, accomplishments, and love were placed in man by God, within temperament areas of Inclusion, Control, and Affection.

Since the beginning of time, man has gone through the same behavior. He can swing back and forth between serving God and serving himself or serving God and man. This can never be done at the same time.

The temperament needs of Affection cannot be met without a deep, emotionally close relationship with God. This emotional intimacy can only be fulfilled by a free association — an association in which man feels free to show and accept God's love.

Drs. Richard and Phyllis Arno

Relationship To God The Father
And The Lord Jesus Christ
Inclusion—Control—Affection
❧ 9 ☙

We have stated several times how our individual temperament affects our interaction with God. The reason for this is the same as with all our other interpersonal relationships. The temperament need we are trying to meet, at the time, will influence how we interact with God at that time.

If we are dealing with God in the area of Inclusion, then our relationship will be geared toward meeting our Inclusion needs. We will only allow God to associate with us in this need area for socialization and surface relationships.

In the area of Control, we can either try to exhibit the need to control God by praying and demanding that God give us what we want, or we can submit control of our lives to God and let Him control us. A person cannot submit to God and submit to self at the same time. We will either let God control us, or we will try to control God. We can either serve ourselves or serve God, but this cannot be done at the same time. We are, of course, called to serve man. John 15:13 states: "Greater love hath no man than this, that a man lay down his life for his friends," but, because of the complexities of temperament, we cannot serve both man and God at the same time. We will serve man for the sake of man, or we will serve man for the sake of God and for the advancement of His Kingdom.

In the area of Affection, people will naturally express (give and receive) love and affection to God in the same manner as they express love and affection to others. If they resist opening up and establishing deep relationships with others, they will also resist a deep intimate relationship with God. The temperament needs of Affection cannot be fully met without a deep, emotionally close relationship with our Creator. This emotional intimacy can only be fulfilled by a free association in which a person feels free to accept God's love and to express their love for Him.

The Five Temperament Types
❧ 10 ❧

*J*n this chapter, we want to introduce you to five (not four) temperament types and to provide you with some basic knowledge and understanding of the strengths and weaknesses of each temperament type, when it is identified in the three specific areas of human behavior, i.e., Inclusion, Control Affection. An introduction is as follows:

Melancholy

Inclusion

A Melancholy expresses or shows the need to socialize or associate with very few people in the area of surface relationships.

Melancholies respond to very few people with a need to associate in surface relationships because they want to associate with very few people and they are very selective.

Control

Melancholies will express or show the need of very little control over other people's lives and responds to or wants very little control over their own life and behavior from others.

Affection Melancholies have the need to express or show very little love and affection, and they only respond to or want very little love and affection.

Choleric

Inclusion

Cholerics express the need for a great deal of self-initiated social interaction, but in the responsive or wanted area they want or need very little association initiated by others.

Control

Cholerics express or show the need to have a great deal of control over other people's lives and behavior, but in the responsive or wanted area they will tolerate almost no control over their own lives and behavior from other people.

Affection

Cholerics express or show a high need for love, affection, approval and deep relationships; however, they accept it only on their own terms.

Sanguine

Inclusion

A Sanguine expresses or shows the need for a great deal of association or social contact. In the responsive or wanted control area, the Sanguine needs to be approached by a great many people for association.

Control

Sanguines express or show the need for a great deal of control over other people's behavior. They also respond to or want controlover their life and behavior by other people when in their dependent swing. This is, however, a very temporary dependency.

The Sanguine in Control is rare, and it is found in only 2% ofthe entire population, predominantly male. The Sanguine in Control has an independent/dependent conflict. At this point it is not important that the reader understand this because it will be discussed later in the book. It is only important that the reader recognizes the Sanguine's control needs.

Affection

Sanguines express or show a great deal of love and affection. In the responsive or wanted affection area, they want a great deal of love and affection from the people around them.

Supine

Inclusion

Supines express or show the need for very little association and socialization, yet the responsive or wanted need is to be approached by many people for association. They want to be included; however, others are never aware of their need. This is called "indirect" behavior.

Control

Supines express or show the need for very little control over the lives of others, but respond or want people around them to take a great deal of control over their life.

Affection

In the temperament need for love and affection (expresses the need for) the Supine shows very little love and affection, but respond to or want a great deal of love and affection from other people.

Phlegmatic

Inclusion

The Phlegmatic expresses or shows only a moderate amount of association or socialization and responds to or wants only a moderate amount of association and socialization.

Control

Phlegmatics express or show only a moderate amount of control over other people's lives and want or are willing to accept only a moderate amount of control over their own lives.

Affection

The Phlegmatic expresses or shows a moderate amount of love and affection and responds to or wants only a moderate amount of love and affection.

The Five Temperaments
And Spiritual Growth
✷ 11 ✷

Because of the five temperaments and their blendings, the spiritual growth of each individual is different. Temperaments and needs within temperaments determine the level and freedom of interaction with God the Father and the Lord Jesus Christ. Temperaments determine how free we are to respond to His love and how openly we worship Him. Temperament is also the determining factor in how exuberant we are in worship, and determines which of us will accept the love, joy, and peace God gives us or how we will reject it because of feelings of worthlessness.

We have already pointed out that our relationship to God is an interpersonal relationship. Our temperament needs of Inclusion, Control, and Affection are the needs that must be met when interacting with people. These needs must also be met in our relationship and interaction with God.

When a person goes to God in prayer, worships Him in a church, or talks to Him as a friend, he or she does this to meet an emotional need. When the emotional need has been met, the spiritual relationship grows. For example, if the Sanguine interacts in the area of love and affection, then he or she will need to show God a great deal of love and affection. He or she will also demand a lot of love and affection in return.

When Cholerics interact with God in the area of Control, they will want to control God through behaviors designed to control Him. They will not submit to God unless there is no other option and, even at that, they will be using God to get something. The Choleric is a user of people. In terms of temperament, however, being a people user is not a weakness. It is only a weakness when one uses people, God, or His Word to manipulate and control people, regardless of their individual rights and feelings. Basically, all people attempt to use God for some purpose. Salvation is the act of receiving the Lord Jesus Christ as our personal Savior by appropriating the blood of Christ as a way to have sins forgiven and to obtain eternal life now and a future home in Heaven. When energized by the Holy Spirit, the Choleric will realize great accomplishments for the Kingdom of God.

If the Supine is interacting with God in the area of Affection, he or she will show very little love to God, but will demand a great deal of love and affection from Him.

If a Melancholy is interacting with God in the area of Control, he or she will want very little control of God, but will also only allow God to take a minimum amount of control over him or her. You can see how temperament can either enhance or block spiritual growth.

As you can see, achieving a close relationship with God is of paramount importance, but this is almost impossible without the in-depth knowledge of your temperament.

Temperament Strengths
And Weaknesses
❧ 12 ☙

Man was created perfect, but since the fall of Adam every human has been born imperfect. We have spiritual imperfections, physical imperfections, and temperament weaknesses. In each temperament and within each of the temperament need areas, there are perfections (strengths) and imperfections (weaknesses).

The strengths of temperament give us the ability to achieve great things. The cities that are built, the songs that are written, the portraits that are painted, the thousands who come to know the Lord, and the ministry to the multitudes are all expressions of man's temperament strengths. Man uses his temperament strengths for his own purposes and accomplishes great things; however, when he surrenders his rights to the Lord, then God uses an individual's temperament strengths for Kingdom purposes.

A temperament weakness is that part of man which we like to refer to as one of our "crosses to bear." Temperament weaknesses cause us to do the things that we detest in others. However, the same weaknesses also give us the ability to gain a greater dependency on God and show others His glory and power. The glory and power is shown to us each time a weakness threatens to hinder our journey to the "promised land." However; if we ask, God will give us the wisdom to overcome that weakness and complete our journey.

There are some Christians who believe that once the Holy Spirit is in their lives, temperament weaknesses are changed so they no longer hinder them in their work for the Lord. We do not accept this premise. As a result of years of research and observation, we conclude that temperament weaknesses are part of man, regardless of spiritual closeness to God. These weaknesses cannot be controlled or brought under God's ordinances unless we seek and accept God's help every day. Through the freedom of choice, man has been given the ability to sink to his weaknesses or rise to his strengths. With an understanding of our strengths and weaknesses and submission to God, we can bring great glory to Him. Weaknesses are man's reaction to his unmet needs.

Peoples' relationship with God can be severely damaged because they fall prey to one of their temperament weaknesses. They know their behavior is displeasing to God, yet they have no idea how to overcome it. After a short while, they perceive themselves to be worthless Christians and withdraw from God. With the temperament information we can provide, we are able to help reverse the process. For example, the Melancholy becomes angry and fights back each time he is confronted for his mistakes. Since anger is perceived to be displeasing to God, Melancholies feel they cannot be good Christians because of the anger they feel. Therefore, Melancholies will withdraw from God. Once the temperament is identified, the person learns how to deal with this weakness and a growing spiritual experience is facilitated.

Pure Temperament Types

❧ 13 ❧

*I*n order to provide you with a deeper understanding of human behavior, we need to go to the foundation of each temperament, to the pure temperament types.

There are nine temperament types. However, there are only five pure temperament types. The asterisks denote the pure types.

1. The Melancholy

2. The Melancholy compulsive

3. The Choleric

4. The Choleric compulsive

5. The Sanguine

6. The Sanguine compulsive

7. The Supine

8. The Supine compulsive

9. The Phlegmatic

As we explain each of the temperaments, we will not attempt to separate the compulsive areas. That is to say, the compulsive will be included within the pure temperament type explanation.

As we take this deeper look into human behavior, we must reiterate two important points:

1. Very few persons are pure in any temperament.

2. Temperament is not actual behavior.

People can be Melancholies, but they can behave as if they are a Sanguine. All this actually tells us is that they are stressed to the maximum within their temperament identity.

It is unlikely that a person within a compulsive temperament area could behave any differently from what his or her actual test scores indicate. When people are compulsive, their compulsion has an extremely deep hold on their behavior; i.e., it is nearly impossible for them to behave any differently.

Each temperament has vital need areas. To give you an example, the following is presented:

Human beings are like flowers.

A flower must have water. Each flower has need of a different amount of water. That is, some need water every day, and some flowers would die if watered every day. Human beings are the same way.

As a Christian, it is vital for you to:

a. Identify your needs.
b. Identify the extent of your needs.
c. Find ways to meet your needs in a godly manner.

It would be virtually impossible to cover each and every possible combination of temperament blends because there are thousands and thousands of combinations. Therefore, in the following chapters we will only deal with the pure temperament types, i.e., those individuals who are the same temperament in all three areas: Inclusion, Control, and Affection. As stated earlier, most individuals are not the same temperament in all three areas; however, this will provide us with a "track to run on" so we can teach you about human behavior from a Christian perspective, i.e., spiritual genetics.

Drs. Richard and Phyllis Arno

The Melancholy

~ 14 ~

Melancholy in Inclusion

This section covers the temperament needs for social interaction, surface relationships, and intellectual energies.

Melancholies are plagued all of their lives by low self-esteem and the fear of rejection because they do not like themselves. No other temperament can focus in on their imperfections and shortcomings better than the Melancholies. Their inadequacies are usually only in their own mind and are not how others perceive them, yet low self-esteem causes this person to constantly search the environment for messages to confirm this low self-image. Fear of rejection causes Melancholies to reject others first when they perceive that they could be rejected. They project their negative attitude of themselves onto others and subconsciously do and say things that will force the negative response they expect.

Melancholies in Inclusion are loners, very introverted and unsure of themselves; however, on the surface they appear to be competent and in control. They also can appear to be arrogant, withdrawn, aloof-looking down their noses at you. In social settings, their behavior is very direct. They can be friendly and personable, depending on the circumstances and how comfortable (accepted) they feel.

When Melancholies suffer from problems, they are usually deeper emotional problems such as depression, stress and fear. Melancholies do not engage in histrionic (emotional, theatrical) behavior. If a Melancholy attempts suicide, he or she will probably succeed. Melancholies seldom tell people of their intentions. They commit suicide because in their mind it is the rational alternative to a painful and difficult life they can no longer face. Whereas if a Sanguine threatens or attempts suicide he or she is probably not serious—they are doing it for attention.

Hippocrates referred to the Melancholy as the "black temperament." No other color can describe this temperament better, for no other temperament is so tormented by "black moods" as the Melancholy in Inclusion. Persons who are Melancholies can be thrown into a deep, black depression by their thinking processes alone. The Melancholy mind is always working, always churning, and the amount of energy this thinking process generates is phenomenal. When this mental energy is focused on negatives, it can do terrible things to a person. When Melancholies begin thinking about how worthless their life is, or how people are out to get them, or that the world is against them, etc., the Melancholy's mood will follow the thoughts downward. As long as these thoughts are spiraling downward, so too will their moods. This depression can last hours, days, weeks, or months. When the person is in this deep depression, suicide is not outside the realm of possible behavior. These "black moods" have caused many Melancholies to go into a self-destruct mode to the point where they will resort to destructive behavior. This can result in alcoholism, drug addiction, sexual addiction, and suicide. No other temperament is more likely to destroy themselves or is more apt to separate themselves from God because of their feelings of worthlessness.

When Melancholies' thought processes swing upward, based on how good their lives are, how much they are loved by the people around them, or how God has blessed them, their mood will also swing upward. They will not be as outgoing as Sanguines, but they will be much happier people. However, their thinking must be harnessed and directed upward.

When it comes to physical ailments caused by emotional disturbances, Melancholies are the most plagued. High blood pressure, ulcers, heart disease, insomnia, and a host of other physical ailments are frequently a part of their plight.

As you can see, the life of the Melancholy in Inclusion is not often a happy one. You may wonder why God would give someone a temperament that would make a person as miserable as this, but our minds are not the mind of God.

The Melancholy also has more profound Inclusion strengths than any other temperament. If you have ever read a novel you simply could not put down, marveled at an oil painting, been captivated by a sculpture, or been enthralled by a piece of music, then you were most likely viewing the work of a Melancholy. No other temperament is more artistic or is more genius-prone than is the Melancholy. The Melancholy is constantly searching and digging, trying to learn new things and unlock the secrets of the universe. Things to challenge the intellect are boundless, and, once the door is unlocked for this wisdom and knowledge, the door will never be closed. If you know a person who prays and seeks the gifts of wisdom and understanding, then you probably know a Melancholy. In the Bible Moses, Solomon and John appeared to be very strong Melancholies, and we know the great truths that came from these three men.

There is, however, a problem with the wisdom and knowledge with which Melancholies have been gifted; they are reluctant to share it because of their low self-esteem. Their introversion and their fear of being wrong and making a mistake causes them to hoard what they know. They are strong-minded and strong-willed, and penetration of that strong mind and will must be accomplished intellectually.

Melancholies have a tendency to be task oriented, not relationship oriented. They relate better to jobs to be done than to people. They do not naturally understand what it is like to build a relationship but do understand what it is like to do a job. In fact, their entire life is a job to do, always with an end result in mind. When taking on a task, they not only have a very good mind for seeing the finished product but also have an ability to see all the potential pitfalls. Melancholies work at a slow, steady pace, losing momentum as the day progresses.

Melancholies are perfectionists and set standards for themselves and others no one can live up to. They do not ask someone to do something they would not do themselves; however, the standards they require are almost impossible to meet. This contributes to their low self-esteem. They can never quite feel they have done a task well enough.

The Melancholy can be very easily insulted and hurt, but when you look at them you will not know it (unless they want you to know). They have an emotional score card they keep in their heads. On this card they keep track of all the things which they perceive you have done to them. Every time you reject them, insult them, or hurt them it is added to that score card. Eventually you will do one more thing and, when that last thing is added, they react in a fit of anger, throwing everything back at you. To the person on the receiving end of this anger, it seems like an overreaction, but to Melancholies, this anger is justified. They are not reacting to just this one incident but rather to all incidents in the past.

If spouses want to make Melancholies comfortable, they should work very hard to give them an orderly, stable home in which to live. Where the Sanguine likes to go to parties and be with people, the Melancholy is a homebody. Melancholies consider their home to be a sanctuary away from the pressures of the world, a place where they can be themselves without fear of being rejected or hurt. Melancholies can only regenerate by being alone and quiet, at which time they can think, dream and shut out the rest of the world. This makes life very difficult for the spouse and children of Melancholies. When they come home after a long day's work, their spouses and children want their time and attention, but they are just too tired to respond. At this point the Melancholy needs quiet time alone in which to regenerate.

Melancholy children are the hardest to raise. They are so sensitive that a parent can injure them deeply without thinking. They can be driven to drugs and alcohol to counteract the pain a parent has inflicted on them.

Regardless of all the weaknesses the Melancholy may suffer, the Melancholy, when energized by the Holy Spirit, has the capabilities of doing a great deal of good in the Kingdom of God. Extremely persistent, self-sacrificing people, they will work relentlessly to bring about changes for the betterment of mankind. When you see the missionary living in a hovel and crying for unsaved souls and starving children, then you are most likely watching a Melancholy. If someone is manning a suicide hotline late into the night, going without sleep and living on coffee, you are probably watching a Melancholy. If you see a person who will suffer indignities and humiliations to bring the Word of God to a backward country, then you are most likely seeing the work of a Spirit-controlled Melancholy.

Anger is common to the Melancholy in Inclusion. Melancholies become angry if they cannot live up to their own standards and if others cannot live up to them. If they have been rejected or hurt, they become angry; this anger is very deep-seated. This person is a great grudge holder; Melancholies get mad, then they get even, or they take vengeance on the person who wronged them. With their intellectual capacities, Melancholies can be very ingenious when it comes to getting revenge.

Melancholies in Inclusion are also thinkers. Their minds never shut off. They can see pictures in their mind in perfect detail and living color. This ability to see things can lead the Melancholy to have fantasies, both sexual and romantic. In these fantasies the relationships are so perfect that real life could not possibly live up to it, and they are let down. The Melancholy in Inclusion is very moody; their thought process brings their moods up and down. The Melancholy mind is extremely tough. Once the mind is made up, it is almost impossible to change it. However, it also has a great thirst for knowledge. Once this thirst has been uncovered, it is almost unquenchable. The more they learn, the more they want to learn; the more they discover, the more they need to discover. The person who has this kind of intellectual powers can also appear rude when you are talking to them. Melancholies are not really rude; it is just that they are thinkers. You will say or do something that will start their mind working, and they will wander off in thought, totally oblivious to what you are saying.

Melancholy in Inclusion Strengths

In the area of Inclusion, the Melancholy has some very definite strengths which, when controlled, can cause the Melancholy to do many great and wonderful things. These strengths include: introvert, loner, great thinker, genius-prone, very artistic and creative, often found alone in thought, perfectionistic, slow-paced, great understanding of tasks and systems, a critical and challenging mind, and seeing both the pitfalls and the end results of a project undertaken. You can see that once these strengths are brought under the ordinances of God, the Melancholy in Inclusion is capable of great things.

Melancholy in Inclusion Weaknesses

When Melancholies sink to their weaknesses, the following will happen: they become extremely moody, suffer from "black" depressions, reject people, set standards neither they nor anyone else can meet, develop habits that are very hard to break, have suicidal tendencies, low self-esteem and are pessimistic. Therefore, when Melancholies sink to their weaknesses, they can be destructive to themselves and others.

Melancholies have a fear of economic failure that prevents them from going forward. This can also be a strength in that they are thrifty and live within their means.

These are the temperament traits that are present in every person who is a Melancholy in Inclusion, regardless of his or her Control and Affection areas.

Melancholy in Control

This section covers the temperament needs for decision-making abilities, willingness to take on responsibilities, and the need for independence.

The person with the Melancholy in Control makes very good decisions and takes on responsibilities in known or familiar areas. When Melancholies are required to make decisions or take on responsibilities in unknown or unfamiliar areas, they procrastinate, become angry and rebel. Melancholies have very good leadership capabilities, especially if they are allowed to move into these unknown areas at their own speed.

Melancholies in Control are highly independent people and will tolerate very little interference in their lives; on the other hand, they will interfere very little in other people's lives. Melancholies in Control have a hard time submitting to authority because of their high degree of independence. They are also very strong-willed, often seen as a "rebel."

On the surface the person who is a Melancholy in the Control area must appear to be competent and in control.

This need to look competent is much more important than the need to be in control. This mask they are compelled to wear hides either real or imagined inadequacies. They have a fear of being wrong, making mistakes, being discovered to be inadequate, or making a fool of themselves. If you confront Melancholies for making mistakes, or if they are made to look foolish, they become very angry. Melancholies also become very anxious if someone is their sole responsibility.

Melancholy in Control Strengths

When rising to their strengths, persons with the Melancholy in Control are capable of wonderful things. The strengths of this Melancholy are: good decisions-making capabilities, ability to take responsibility in known areas, and very good leadership ability—if allowed to deal in known areas or handle things at their own speed. They adhere to the rules, and they need very little control over the lives and behavior of others.

Melancholy in Control Weaknesses

When Melancholies in Control sink to their weaknesses, they are capable of the following destructive behavior: rigidity, inflexibility, sensitivity to failure, fear of the unknown, fear of failure, rebelliousness and procrastination.

These are the temperament traits that are present in all people who are Melancholies in Control, regardless of their Inclusion and Affection areas.

Melancholy in Affection

This section covers the need for love and affection, and the need for deep personal relationships.

Melancholies in Affection, show very little love and affection and needs very little love and affection shown to them by others. Melancholies approach very few people for deep personal relationships, and the deep personal relationships they do establish are very few and far between.

Once these deep personal relationships have been established, Melancholies are very faithful, loyal friends. Melancholies have the capacity to be extremely self-sacrificing for deep personal friends and mankind in general, yet they are also the most vengeful. If they are hurt or rejected by a deep personal relationship, Melancholies become angry and may go to great lengths to gain revenge.

This person may have extremely low self-esteem. They may not love themselves, and so they do not understand how anyone else can love them. This makes them feel unworthy of anyone's love or acceptance. If they are around anyone who shows too much love or affection, Melancholies are highly distrustful. They are always looking below the surface for hidden reasons why others show them love and affection. Because of these feelings that are so easily hurt, Melancholies very seldom show their deep, inner self. Their lives are already so pain-filled, they feel that if they show these tender feelings it will only give someone a weapon to use to hurt them. They are the most emotionally guarded temperament. On the surface the Melancholy appears to be a distant, cold person, but this hides a very tender heart that can empathize and feel the pain of others. God has truly blessed Melancholies with deep, tender feelings, but they have great difficulty in allowing these feelings to show.

When it comes to loneliness, Melancholies know this emotion all too well because they do not show their tender feelings. The law of reciprocity (the more love you give, the more love you receive) does not come into play. Melancholies do not show love, so they do not receive love. This causes Melancholies to be extremely lonely. The loneliness can be stopped if Melancholies do three things.

First: They must develop a close personal relationship with God, love God, and feel secure in God's love.

Second: They must develop a close personal relationship in which they would actually give up their life for that person.

Third: They must find a way to show those gentle feelings and their love for people and mankind in general by good works. Since Melancholies do not have the mechanism to show affection in physical ways (other than sex), they can express these feelings by practical means of service to others.

Melancholy in Affection Strengths

The Melancholy in Affection has strengths that can lead them to great accomplishments. Melancholies are faithful and loyal friends and self-sacrificing. Their feelings run deep and tender (even though they lack the ability to express these feelings). Melancholies can easily empathize with others and have the ability to make deep commitments.

Melancholy in Affection Weaknesses

When Melancholies in Affection sink to their weaknesses, they become destructive to themselves and their deep relationships. They dissect the past with theoretical "what ifs," i.e., "what if" he had given me flowers, I would feel loved; "what if" I were prettier, they would love me more. Also, they are critical of others, angry, cruel, vengeful, emotional, rarely tell people how they feel, have a low self-image and are sensitive to rejection.

The loss of a deep relationship (close friend, spouse, family, etc.) is devastating to the Melancholy in Affection. This is viewed as a weakness because they never seem to be able to recover. It is a deep emotional scar that remains throughout their lives.

The major weakness of Melancholies in Affection is that they are sexually oriented but not romantically inclined. They "have sex" with their spouse; they do not "make love" to them. This causes a lot of marital problems.

These are the temperament traits that are present in each

person who is a Melancholy in Affection, regardless of his or her Inclusion and Control areas.

The Melancholy Relationship To God

Hopefully, the Melancholy (pure, i.e., Melancholy in Inclusion, Control and Affection) is introduced to God in childhood. The older the Melancholy is, the harder he/she is to reach. The Melancholy is easily habituated and, once a habit has been developed, it is almost impossible to break. Once they have developed the habit of living without God's help, it is almost impossible to motivate them to change this habit and start to depend on God. Once the introduction has been made, the Melancholy believes that God must meet certain needs before they will associate with Him. To the Melancholy, God must be orderly, reliable, and dependable. God must also want a free association and accept them just the way they are. If God does not meet these criteria, they will be extremely critical of Him and will not let the relationship go any further. In the Inclusion area, Melancholies must be able to intellectualize their relationship with God. Because much of the Christian religion must be accepted on faith, we should not let Melancholies intellectualize this relationship. If Melancholies are encouraged to ask questions and search for answers, they will go to the next level of interaction within their temperament.

The next area that God works on is the temperament need of Control. If the Melancholy has been taught that God manipulates us and forces us to submit by rewarding good behaviors and punishing bad, then the Melancholy will rebel, never allowing Christ into the deepest recesses of his or her heart. If the Melancholy in Control understands that God allows us free choice of will and will never go against that will, there is no reason for rebellion. The Melancholy does not respond to the threat of punishment nor the promise of reward as motivation to make changes. Melancholies will only change if they make the choice freely.

If Melancholies believe that God knows and understands their need for independence, their need to keep control of their own life, and that the ultimate choice belongs to them, then Melancholies will allow God into the deepest recesses of their heart.

The Melancholy must then find Jesus. Jesus is the deep personal relationship for which this temperament yearns. Melancholies can actually feel and empathize with the pain Christ went through and the sacrifice of His death. He is the "Friend that sticketh closer than a brother" to whom the Melancholy can freely bare his or her soul.

Because of the temperament traits of Melancholies, if they feel they are being forced into showing love for Christ in ways in which they are not comfortable, then this love for Christ will be held only in their hearts. However, if this person is encouraged to show their love for Christ in ways in which they are comfortable, they will become a self-sacrificing worker for the Lord. If Melancholies are allowed to work for Christ as their way of showing love and affection, their relationship will continue to grow. If Melancholies believe they must demonstrate their love and affection in ways such as speaking in front of large groups, becoming very emotional, or doing other things that force them too far out of their temperament, these expressions will not come about publicly, but their love for Christ will be only in their heart.

Major Temperament Needs of the Melancholy

The following is a list of the basic needs of a person who is a Melancholy in Inclusion, Control and Affection (commonly referred to as a pure Melancholy).

1. To have quiet, alone time—to regenerate.

2. To have a limited amount of interaction with people—to be free from required socialization.

3. To be creative.

4. To work with tasks and systems.

5. To have everything in order — they require perfection — of self and others.

6. To fill their thirst for knowledge.

7. To have financial and economic security.

8. To be accepted and have approval.

9. To appear competent and in control.

10. To have truth, order, reliability and dependability.

11. To have independence — they do not like to be controlled or manipulated.

12. To be free from romantic demands — they are sexually oriented but not romantically oriented. They need very little romance such as holding hands and walking under a starlit sky.

13. To have facts. They have a fear of looking foolish in unknown areas and need to be cautious before moving forward, e.g., read the instructions.

Special Things That Significant Others Can Do For The Melancholy

1. Provide them with truth, order, reliability and dependability.

2. Work very hard at helping to raise their self-esteem by reinforcing the positive and downplaying the negative within the environment.

3. Allow them quiet time alone in order to regenerate.

4. Show them that they are loved and appreciated, displaying only minimal amounts of physical attention. Otherwise, they will feel crowded. The best way to show this individual you love and appreciate them is by doing "special" things or tasks, such as washing windows, putting oil in the car, or helping them with housework.

5. Do not interfere with their independence or what they are self-motivated to do or accomplish.

6. Provide them with a home that is orderly and acts as a sanctuary away from the rest of the world.

7. Do not make them feel foolish, criticize them, or confront them for their mistakes.

8. Do not force them to take on responsibilities or make decisions in "new" areas where they are not comfortable until they have had ample time for this to become a "known area."

9. Do not force them to take on the sole responsibility for someone else.

10. Be careful with money and show that you are attempting to be conservative with money.

11. Encourage them to develop habits and to do the same things at the same time every day. This will add to their efficiency.

12. Assist them in finding employment in areas where they can undertake tasks with a minimal amount of interaction with people or the general public.

13. Help them to learn how to deal with anger constructively instead of destructively.

14. Help them focus their minds on positive things, thinking on things that are good instead of things that are negative. This will lessen their moodiness and depression.

15. Help them learn how to replace bad habits with good habits, how to recognize their mistakes and learn from the past mistakes so they will not repeat them.

16. Encourage them to show or express their deep and tender feelings in ways that are comfortable to them and to those they love.

What Melancholies Can Do To Help Themselves

1. Deal with anger constructively.

2. Give others and themselves the right to be imperfect.

3. Forgive themselves and others for past mistakes.

4. Find life situations where they can provide themselves with the quiet time alone they need every day.

5. Provide themselves with life situations where they can undertake tasks that have a minimal amount of interaction with people.

6. Find employment where they can work one steady shift. This will add to their efficiency.

7. Develop habits of doing the same things at the same time every day to reach optimum productive potential.

8. Keep their minds focused on the positive things in their lives in order to lessen moodiness.

9. Show deep, tender feelings in ways that are comfortable to them and that others can understand.

10. Replace bad habits with good habits.

11. Maintain proper level of work, relaxation, diet and exercise.

12. Challenge intellectual energies in times of stress by reading, working, or other pursuits. This will also help break the downward thinking process.

13. Do not force themselves to socialize often or for long periods of time.

14. Develop a deep personal relationship for which they would give up their lives. This will lessen loneliness.

15. Focus their minds on the way people show their love for them instead of the ways they do not.

Behavior Changes That Bring Melancholies Closer To God

1. Forgive old, painful memories. Each time they are recalled, they need to remember that they forgave these things.

2. Focus on what God has given them and develop a thankful attitude. This will lessen moodiness.

3. Become secure in the love of God. They need to know they are worthy of His love. This will raise their self-perception and make them less fearful of rejection.

4. Trust God to unlock their potential. They may rebel against what God wants them to do, especially in unknown areas.

5. Develop a deep loving relationship with Christ to prevent sexual sins such as adultery, fornication and romantic fantasies.

6. Lessen criticism by looking at others with the eyes of Christ, giving them permission to be imperfect.

7. Forgive themselves for past failures. They will beat themselves to death over mistakes.

8. Follow God into the unknown to reduce their fear. They will fear the unknown to the point where it will immobilize them.

9. Make themselves the best they can be according to the limits God has provided them. Then, if they are rejected, offended, or insulted because of this, it is not their problem but that of the other person. They will find insult, offense, and rejection where none is meant. This fuels the circle of anger and vengeance.

10. Make their lives pleasing to God and not society. They will feel guilty if they do not measure up to the standards set by society or their families.

Drs. Richard and Phyllis Arno

The Choleric

≈ 15 ≈

Choleric in Inclusion

This section covers the temperament needs for social interaction, surface relationship, and intellectual energies.

When we observe an individual who is highly personable and charming, as is a Sanguine, but does not like people, we are looking at a Choleric in Inclusion. Like a Sanguine, a Choleric in Inclusion is a person who can inspire great numbers of people.

At a party or in a social setting the Choleric, on the surface, is highly personable, optimistic, and well-liked. Cholerics can be very charming, open and friendly to most of the people around them. Associates and people they meet at parties or social gatherings respond well to their charm. To the Choleric, people are not persons, they are "tools" to be used. The Choleric will associate only with those "tools" that can be used. Parties, socializing, and associations will be chosen that will help Cholerics reach their goals.

The Choleric in Inclusion has a personable, almost arrogant manner in dealing with people, and most of us would believe they are genuine in relating to people. However, the Choleric is a task oriented person. The real interaction that Cholerics attempt to establish is for their driving need for accomplishments and recognition for their accomplishments. Cholerics approach very many people for surface relationships because people are necessary to complete a project and they must be easily dominated and used. Quite possibly, the Choleric is capable of using people, even walking over them to reach the end results.

Cholerics have one of the worst tempers, and they have the intellectual ability to use this temper against the people around them who displease them. This temper is usually cruel and abusive. When unleashed, it is used to hurt people.

The Choleric in Inclusion is a fast-paced individual who undertakes projects quickly and efficiently. Because of their intellectual energies, Cholerics are very good at envisioning new projects. They have a very difficult time seeing any of the possible pitfalls which lie ahead. If they are a Choleric in the Control area of temperament, they will undoubtedly carry the project through to the end. Cholerics are perfectionistic and will question the means and the methods of the people around them. Cholerics believe they know "a better way to do it."

Cholerics in Inclusion need almost constant recognition for their accomplishments and will become angry if they do not receive this recognition.

Choleric in Inclusion Strengths

In the temperament area of Inclusion the Choleric has some excellent strengths, which include being open, friendly, confident, outgoing, optimistic and tough-minded. This person is perfectionistic and has a good mind for envisioning new projects and is an extrovert of a highly selective nature.

Choleric in Inclusion Weaknesses

In the temperament area of Inclusion, the Choleric also has some weaknesses. Cholerics are often hot-tempered and, although everyone uses people to some extent, the Choleric in Inclusion "carries the flag." They are people users, however, they call themselves "people motivators." In addition, because of being easily frustrated in their attempts to "motivate" people, Cholerics harbor anger and are sometimes cruel.

Cholerics in Inclusion have another weakness which they view as a strength, they always dominate social conversations. Cholerics are not necessarily rude, just domineering in all social interaction. They control the social scene.

These temperament traits are present in each person who is a Choleric in Inclusion, regardless of his or her Control and Affection areas.

Choleric in Control

This section covers the temperament needs for decision-making abilities, willingness to take on responsibilities, and the need for independence.

When making decisions and taking on responsibilities, the Choleric does very well and has excellent leadership abilities. Cholerics make quality decisions and handle responsibilities that would make other temperaments run away. Those decisions are made quickly and intuitively, leaving others in their wake. When responsibilities are undertaken, they are done so in an efficient, well-disciplined, military fashion. No other temperament is as well organized and disciplined as the Choleric. Cholerics also have a knack for choosing people to help them complete the project, people who will do exactly what the Choleric wants.

When carrying through with projects, the Choleric is capable of undertaking any behavior necessary. To them, the end justifies the means. Cholerics will tolerate almost no interference and seldom trust anyone else with projects. This is because they feel that no one else can do it as well as they themselves. Because of this, Cholerics have difficulty delegating authority. They are the temperament most likely to burn themselves out.

Cholerics need almost constant recognition for their accomplishments and will become angry if they do not receive adequate recognition.

Cholerics in Control need a great deal of control over other people's lives and behavior but will accept very little control over their own lives and behavior from others. If Cholerics relate to people and want relationships with people, then they will have to control those people with whom they associate. The Choleric in Control has very little idea of how to handle people other than through domination. The people around Cholerics are always seeking encouragement because they are in awe of them. But instead of encouragement, they receive put-downs and discouraging remarks. The Cholerics in Control surround themselves with weak-willed and easily-dominated individuals. In time, the Choleric in Control begins to dislike and lose respect for others because of their weaknesses. Cholerics hold weak-willed people in contempt and begin treating them cruelly. On the other hand, Cholerics have a difficult time working with a strong-willed person they cannot control and with whom they usually become angry.

Choleric in Control Strengths
The strengths of a Choleric in Control include being tough-willed, a good leader, capable of making intuitive decisions based on facts rather than feelings, capable of taking on responsibilities, and possessing the will power to carry things through to completion.

Choleric in Control Weaknesses
Weaknesses of the Choleric in Control include anger, cruelty, capability of undertaking any behavior to keep

control, associating with weak people, and resenting their weaknesses.

These are the temperament traits that are present in each person who is a Choleric in Control, regardless of his or her Inclusion and Affection areas.

Choleric in Affection

This section covers the temperament need for love and affection, and the need for deep personal relationships.

This person is a bright, optimistic, affectionate person who appears to be a Sanguine. Cholerics in Affection appear to want deep personal relationships, but in reality do not. When approached for love and affection they will most likely turn their back, and when approached for a deep personal relationship they will walk away from it. The explanation for this is very simple; they must be shown love and affection according to their terms. They will not accept a deep personal relationship if their terms are not met.

The Choleric in Affection seems to have very few emotions and feelings other than anger. They are extremely self-centered people, and the needs, wants, and desires of other people do not count. The total drive of this temperament is to have their own wants and desires met while disregarding the emotions of other people as useless sentimentalism.

To the Choleric, compassion, tenderness, and warmth are generally considered a waste of time. If this person ever develops any feelings or emotions, it is because of the direct intervention of God.

Choleric in Affection Strengths

In the temperament area of Affection, Choleric strengths include being open, optimistic, outgoing, they express a great deal of love and affection, and approach only select people for deep relationships.

Choleric in Affection Weaknesses

In the temperament area of Affection, Choleric weaknesses include having indirect behavior and rejecting people, rejecting the love and affection of people, and beingcruel to those who reject their manipulation for love and affection.

These temperament traits are present in each person who is a Choleric in Affection, regardless of his or her Inclusion and Control areas.

The Choleric Relationship to God

Like the Melancholy, and even more so, the pure Choleric in Inclusion, Control and Affection needs to develop a strong relationship with God during childhood. In fact, our research indicates that most of the Cholerics who became strong leaders for God were usually raised in the church.

If the person with the Choleric temperament has been raised from childhood with very strong moral values, then his or her behavior will be better. These morals will not be discarded in adulthood. However, if parents do not instill morals or a sense of right and wrong into their Choleric child, the child will grow up as a "cloudy" Choleric. This means that the Cholerics vision of right and wrong and their understanding of good and evil is clouded. Since Cholerics do not have emotions upon which to draw, they will do anything or undertake any behavior to have their own way. This is why the Choleric can become sociopathic. The sociopath has no comprehension of good and evil and, if he or she does possess a conscience, it is seldom, if ever, used and does nothing to alter his or her behavior. When Cholerics reach adulthood (if not raised in the church), they are so self-reliant and confident they think they have no need for God and feel quite comfortable with their lives the way they are. This makes it very difficult to reach Cholerics for Christ.

The very strong Choleric who is reached in adulthood is usually reached by direct intervention of God.

In Apostle Paul's case, he literally had to be struck blind and miraculously healed. After God brought Paul to Himself, He used his temperament traits to do His will. Paul established churches and was able to keep them flourishing, even from a distance. Usually, other Cholerics are reached in ways that are just as miraculous, such as deathbed healings and personal encounters with God. When this happens, you can be sure that God has a very definite plan for the person who has these temperament traits.

God has provided mankind very few pure Choleric temperaments. This temperament has more power and is capable of more destructive force than any of the other temperaments. Some of the world's most feared criminals and terrible dictators have been pure Cholerics. Adolf Hitler and Joseph Stalin possessed Choleric traits.

Adolf Hitler is a good case study of how a person with a Choleric temperament can operate. A small, nondescript man, Hitler inspired a whole country and attempted to control the destiny of the world. Using his social graces and charisma, he positioned men, tools for the Choleric to use, in places of power who would help and not interfere with his plan. A plan as immense and evil as his could not be undertaken without evil men who would follow his dream. Thousands of people who were perceived to taint the pure German blood were systematically eliminated. Hitler did not even say "kill or murder"; they were not people to him, only "things" to be eliminated. The pure Cholerics have almost no emotions, so they feel no pain, no remorse, no guilt. Since Hitler felt no love, compassion, tenderness or gentleness, he felt nothing for the men, women, and children who were eliminated. They were only inconveniences that stood between him and his ultimate goal. This plan was evil and unattainable, but this did not deter Hitler. He had the strength of will to carry it through to the end, and if it had not been for God's intervention and World War II, he might have been successful. In a similar example, Stalin systematically set out to imprison and murder millions of Russians. From what you see here, the pure Choleric in this depraved form is the most dangerous of all temperaments. However, God also uses Cholerics for His Kingdom.

To better understand the Choleric, let us look at how this temperament, when matured, interacts with God.

Inclusion:

The Choleric is introduced to God. Cholerics are quite personable and appear to want a relationship with Him, but deep down they will only associate with people they can dominate and use to get what they want. This need to dominate a relationship makes it very difficult for them to develop and enjoy their relationship with God.

Control:

The Choleric must interact with God to the point of not being controlled by God but by controlling Him. This highly independent temperament does not depend on God but depends on themselves. When taking on decisions or responsibilities, Cholerics believe they can do things even better than God.

Affection:

If the above criteria are met, Cholerics then take God into the area of deep personal relationships. In this area, God must be able to be dominated and used. They will show love and affection, but it will be according to their terms and their criteria.

As you can see, for the mature Choleric to develop a deep relationship with God and a personal reliance upon Him, it is a long and difficult process. It is possible for God, by the Holy Spirit, to reach the Choleric and, through a process of breaking and humbling, the Choleric can become a leader in the Kingdom of God.

Major Temperament Needs of the Choleric

The following is a list of the basic needs of a person who is a Choleric in Inclusion, Control and Affection (commonly referred to as a pure Choleric).

1. To have social interaction for the purpose of motivating others and selling their ideas, wares, etc.

2. To make decisions based on facts and to be in control of self and others.

3. To receive recognition for their accomplishments.

4. To receive love and affection on their terms.

5. To achieve and succeed — they are task oriented.

6. To be followed — they are leaders.

7. To have time away from people and socialization.

8. To initiate social interaction — even though they dread the thought of socializing as the time approaches; however, once engaged in social interaction, they have a great time.

9. To have tasks performed correctly — they are efficient and perfectionistic.

Special Things That Significant Others Can Do
For The Choleric

1. Do not force them to socialize.

2. Do not interfere with their independence, try to control them, or tell them what to do.

3. Recognize their need for accomplishments and give them opportunities to meet this need.

4. Recognize their need to make decisions and take on responsibilities. Provide them the opportunity to do so. Others should not interfere with them when they are taking on tasks and responsibilities.

5. Learn the art of negotiation to prevent being dominated by them.

6. Provide them with love and affection according to their needs and desires.

7. Work very hard at showing them they are loved by doing "special things" for them.

8. Render assistance when it is required.

9. Keep emotional outbursts to a minimum.

What Cholerics Can Do To Help Themselves

1. Deal with their anger constructively.

2. Find life situations where they can achieve things and receive recognition for the services they render.

3. Find life situations where their need for accomplishments can be obtained.

4. Recognize the rights and feelings of others.

5. Submit to authority, especially that of the Lord, while maintaining control of their own personal lives.

6. Recognize the needs of others while showing love and affection, that is, not just giving love as a means of manipulation.

7. Trust others and accept them as they are.

8. Delegate responsibility in order to lessen the possibility of burnout.

9. Refrain from using love and affection to control others.

10. Only control others by good behavior, such as love, compassion and encouragement, instead of abusive behavior.

11. Learn how to forgive so they can release pent-up anger and painful memories that can fuel their vengeance.

12. Learn to use the high control God gave them to control themselves, not others.

Behavior Changes That Bring Cholerics Closer to God

1. Forgive old painful memories and replace them with good, joyful ones. This will break the circle of anger and vengeance.

2. Deal with anger constructively. Cholerics will lash out at others with an angry, cruel temper. They must never allow themselves to hurt people physically or emotionally when angry.

3. Submit to God. Cholerics will rebel against God when they believe He is taking too much control of their life. This only breeds misery. Submission unlocks the potential for achievement God has placed within them.

4. Recognize the rights and feelings of others according to the ordinances of God. They will walk over the rights and feelings of others to gain profit and power.

5. Make their behavior pleasing to God. They have a tendency to undertake poor or sinful behaviors to maintain control of other people.

6. Pray for the Fruit of the Spirit, i.e., love, joy, peace, etc. so they can learn to understand and feel the emotions that are lacking in their temperament. They cannot understand or empathize with the deep, tender feelings of others.

7. Dedicate all achievements to God and seek His recognition. This will lessen their dependence on man for recognition.

8. Look at others with the "Eyes of Christ." This will give them permission to be imperfect and lessen criticism.

Conclusion

As you can see after completing this in-depth review of the Choleric's behavior patterns and his or her temperament needs, it is important to understand why Cholerics do what they do and the causal factors of their behavior.

Even though we have taken such a deep and concentrated look at the Choleric, it must be understood that this is not the absolute totality of the Choleric. There are many additional needs and problem areas in the Choleric, but they are minor compared to the ones that we have mentioned in this chapter.

The Sanguine
❧ 16 ☙

Sanguine in Inclusion

This section covers the temperament needs for social interaction, surface relationships, and intellectual energies.

The Sanguine in Inclusion is a social person who likes to be with people. Sanguines are fast paced and the type of people who have their shoes parked at the door and ready to go in a minute. They approach a great many people for surface relationships and associations.

Sanguines in Inclusion are the easiest to identify when in a large group. They are the ones who are the center of attention, talk the loudest, tell the funniest jokes, and wear the brightest colors. Sanguines are responsive to the senses:

sight, smell, taste, touch, and hearing. Hippocrates identified the Sanguine by the color red, or "blood," which fits them perfectly. Sanguines bring life and energy into a room by their very presence. Their cheerfulness and humor brighten everyone's life. When it comes to social orientation, Sanguines in Inclusion are rarely found alone and, if they must be alone, they are talking on the phone, reading a book or watching a TV show about people—anything that will give them the feeling that people are around, and that they are involved in other people's lives. If they are in a situation where they are not able to be with people, Sanguines will find themselves feeling under stress.

When you need someone to inspire and infect people with enthusiasm, you need to find a Sanguine in Inclusion. When you are moved to your knees by an evangelist, you are most likely watching a Sanguine in Inclusion. In the Bible, look at the vast number of people Peter led to Christ; he was probably a Sanguine in Inclusion. Most of the great evangelists we see on TV are more than likely Sanguines in Inclusion. Once their charisma and personality comes into full swing, they can inspire thousands to Christ. When you are lonely, Sanguines are great people to be around. Their bright faces can lift even the loneliest of people. Of all the temperaments, the Sanguine in Inclusion is the easiest to be around socially.

The Sanguine in Inclusion is an optimistic type of person who believes life is an exciting, fun-filled experience that should be lived to the fullest. Inactivity causes Sanguines stress because the pace at which they like to live their lives is fast and furious. Most other temperaments get tired just watching them when they are in full swing. The need to have money at all times is quite typical to the Sanguine in Inclusion. It is not the money itself that they need but what the money represents. As long as they have money in their pockets they can go places and do things with other people! The typical Sanguine in Inclusion loves sales, and is especially vulnerable to things that are colorfully packaged. The Sanguine in

Inclusion is the most impulsive of all the temperaments. Sanguines act and talk before they think through what will happen because of their actions. This is especially true when it comes to money. Sanguines will spend money without worrying where it comes from or for what it might be needed in the future.

The Sanguine in Inclusion excels in communication-oriented things, but becomes impatient with task-oriented jobs. Sanguines do not relate well to tasks but love to relate to people. If they do take a task, it is done as quickly as possible so they can be with people again. Sanguines are the least disciplined and organized of all the temperaments. When relating to people, they are outgoing, enthusiastic, warm, compassionate, and seem to relate well to other people's feelings, yet they can be rude and uncaring. Sanguines will walk away from you when you are in mid-sentence because they are simply not interested in what you have to say anymore, or they will be constantly searching with their eyes to find the next person with whom they will interact. The Sanguine in Inclusion is usually a person we would like to choose as a best friend. This is especially true of the more withdrawn and quiet temperaments. But, the Sanguine in Inclusion is neither a faithful nor loyal friend. They do not want to be "burdened down" with commitments to surface relationships since they just want to have fun.

When an apology is in order, typical Sanguines in Inclusion usually apologize very quickly. At the time, their apology is quite sincere, especially if their behavior causes pain for someone or if the behavior causes them to lose acceptance. However, this apology is short-lived. Since Sanguines in Inclusion live as though they have no past or future, they rarely learn from past mistakes or think about what will happen if those mistakes are repeated.

One of the curiosities of the Sanguine in Inclusion behavior is that he or she is prone to exaggerate. Sanguines exaggerate their emotions, illnesses, health, fun and achievements. They never recognize failures and will exaggerate to make themselves appear more successful than they are. As the exaggerations continue, Sanguines fail to recognize they are lying. To them, they are simply expressing their zest for life.

The Sanguines' major weakness is that they adopt severe and destructive behavior. The two most pronounced behaviors are histrionic behavior and neurotic behavior. Histrionic behavior happens because the Sanguine in Inclusion needs to be the center of attention. Attention is reinforcing or rewarding to this person. So, in essence, when the attention is withheld, Sanguines feel they are being punished. When they undertake good behavior and attention is withheld, to them they are being punished for good behavior. Therefore, Sanguines will undertake bad behavior such as screaming, pouting, crying, or temper tantrums, which usually draw immediate attention. Consistent with principles of reinforcement, Sanguines are thus being rewarded for bad behavior, so this behavior continues. Consequently, the more hysterical the behavior, the more reward or attention they receive.

The second destructive behavior for the Sanguine in Inclusion is neurotic behavior. In neurotic behavior, the needs are different. A person not only needs attention; he or she also need social approval and acceptance. No matter what these persons do, if they do not receive approval, acceptance or attention they feel, in essence, they are being punished for good behavior. They try another route, resorting to bad behavior. Bad behavior starts by lying, cheating, stealing, etc. They receive attention and thus are being rewarded for bad behavior. The behavior continues to get worse and can even escalate to violence. Although attention continues, it is not the type of attention they seek. Primarily, these persons want approval and acceptance but have no idea how to obtain it in the right way. What these Sanguines are creating is the exact opposite of what they really want. Their bad behavior is separating them from the approval and acceptance that they so desperately desire.

Sanguine in Inclusion Strengths

In the temperament area of Inclusion, the Sanguine has some very definite strengths. The temperament strengths of the Sanguine include: being friendly, outgoing, inspiring to others, relationship oriented, enthusiastic, warm, optimistic, ability to see the bright side of life, and the good in other people. Sanguines genuinely like people, are rarely found alone, and freely interact with people. When looking at these strengths, you can see the potential for doing good works for God when Sanguines are brought under God's ordinances.

Sanguine in Inclusion Weaknesses

The weaknesses of a Sanguine in Inclusion are those that can become very destructive to the Sanguine, both emotionally and spiritually. These include: being talkative, always the center of the conversation, apt to take on the behavior and morals of the people around them, impulsive, undisciplined, rude, prone to exaggerate, need to appear successful (even to the point of exaggeration), will ignore responsibilities in order to be with people.

These are the temperament traits that are present in all people who are Sanguine in Inclusion, regardless of their Control and Affection areas.

Sanguine in Control

This section covers the temperament need for decision-making abilities, willingness to take on responsibilities, and the need for in dependence.

Sanguines in Control are somewhat rare. Only a small percent of the population have this Control, and they are predominantly male. The primary problem with Sanguines in Control is that they do not understand themselves and they are not understood by their family, co-workers and friends.

Why is the Sanguine in Control so different from the other temperaments in the Control area? All the other temperaments are stabilized. That is to say, the Melancholy in Control is always independent. The Choleric in Control is always domineering. The Sanguine, on the other hand, SWINGS. Sanguines in Control behave like a Choleric one day, totally in charge and domineering, and the next day they are totally dependent.

When Sanguines in Control are in their independent/ domineering mode, even the Cholerics in Control run for cover. Sanguines in Control are aggressive, responsible, demanding, and capable of undertaking any task. What happens that causes the Sanguine in Control to swing from this "take charge" behavior to the dependent, self-indulging person? The answer is that, when Sanguines in Control are in their dependent swings, they become irresponsible, self-indulgent and, in essence, nearly drown in their own pool of self-pity because they did not receive recognition for their accomplishments.

The Sanguine in Control has an unquenchable need for recognition and approval. If this is withheld by the people whom they consider "important," Sanguines in Control will do a "nose dive." Criticism will also thrust Sanguines in Control into the dependent mode. When they do swing from independent to dependent, they drop everything and shirk their responsibilities. In other words, these persons will volunteer for difficult tasks and they can and will complete the project so long as their ego is being fed. However, at the first sign indicating that they are not "the greatest thing that ever happened to the world," they quit! They just walk away and turn into themselves — caring nothing about the project or those depending upon them.

When Sanguines in Control remain in the dependent, self-indulgent side of their swing for a short period, they begin to feel ugly. This is an emotional "ugly" made up of feelings like guilt, worthlessness, and selfishness. These feelings begin turning them around, and soon they are back to the "take charge," responsible and dependable people everyone knows, loves, and reveres.

We have discovered something amazing about the Sanguine in Control. Unlike the Choleric in Control, who pushes and pushes until he/she goes into total burnout, the Sanguine in Control has a built-in safety value. Sanguines in Control push just as hard as the Cholerics and they accomplish just as much; however, right before they crash and burn, they enter into this temporary dependent/self-indulgent swing. This temporary "all stop" prevents burnout. It is very common for Cholerics in Control to burn themselves out and need months or even years to regenerate. This rarely, if ever, happens to the Sanguine in Control.

Sanguine in Control Strengths and Weaknesses

A Sanguine's strengths and weaknesses correlate with his or her dependent/independent conflict. On one side, Sanguines are driven to control the behavior of the people around them. After taking on too many responsibilities and decisions, they will be driven to the other side of the temperament need, which is to be narcissistic, self-indulgent, lacking persistence, and weak-willed. At the time when the Sanguine manifests independence, he or she will be a solicitous, caring person who will do things for other people, almost to the point of servitude. Sanguines in Control will take on the responsibility for making many decisions to receive recognition. Their need for attention and approval, recognition, and acceptance molds them. Sanguines in Control can be very charming, gracious people; however, they will not stay in this part of the need long. They are endlessly driven back and forth between the two needs like a pendulum. The longer they stay on one side of their temperament, the more they are driven back to the other side. These swings are not strengths or weaknesses, but are temperament needs that must be met. The problem with this narcissistic swing is that Sanguines can indulge themselves in gambling and alcoholic binges, drugs, sexual sins, etc. The need to be self-indulgent is not a weakness, but the way this self-indulgence is met is the weakness. The only thing that can help this Sanguine in Control is to find a life situation where he or she can make a smooth swing from one temperament need to another.

These are the temperament traits that are present in each person who is a Sanguine in Control, regardless of his or her Inclusion and Affection areas.

Sanguine in Affection

This section covers the temperament need for love and affection, and the need for deep personal relationships.

Of all the people in the world, the Sanguine in Affection is the most lovable. Sanguines in Affection express love and affection in an endless supply and will accept as much love and affection as you can show them. When it comes to possessions or things, they care very little about them. Their entire existence is for relating to and establishing deep relationships with people.

The Sanguine in Affection needs to be told every day that he or she is loved, needed, and appreciated. Yesterday's reassurance is gone and tomorrow may never come. Today is the day they need to be loved. This is not to be misinterpreted as a need for sex. This is a need for love, romance, acceptance, approval, and to be touched. The Sanguine in Affection is very sensitive to touch. This need for human contact is a "skin hunger" but not in a sexual sense.

These persons love to hold hands, walk arm in arm, and do anything of a romantic nature with their spouses or loved ones. Sanguines in Affection are the least sexually inhibited. They approach this aspect of marriage by saying; "This is great!" However, it is imperative that the act of sex be an expression of love. Emotional "oneness" is a prerequisite to any sexual act.

The Sanguine in Affection's need to touch and be touched is not limited to the "love partner." Family members can also expect frequent gestures of love. For example, it would not be uncommon for a Sanguine in Affection to stand and rub his or her child's back while talking to him.

The need for touch and being reassured that they are loved is one of the major needs of Sanguines in Affection. However, there is one other major need. This is the need for deep emotional contact. Sanguines in Affection are very quick to reveal their inner selves. They also need for their deep personal relationships to be just as revealing, to open up and share inner feelings, thoughts, and emotions.

Sanguine in Affection Strengths

In the temperament area of Affection, Sanguine strengths include being able to express and receive large amounts of love and affection. Sanguines in Affection are warm, easy to get to know, and emotionally open.

Sanguine in Affection Weaknesses

The weakness in the temperament area of Affection is that Sanguines can be easily devastated if not constantly reassured that they are loved and appreciated. They are very demanding of other people for love and affection and are plagued with feelings of jealousy when the love and attention (that they feel belongs exclusively to them) is given to others.

These are the temperament traits that are present in each person who is a Sanguine in Affection, regardless of his or her Inclusion and Control areas.

The Sanguine Relationship To God

Of all the children to raise, the pure Sanguine in Inclusion, Control, and Affection is the one to which the least amount of emotional harm can be done. Pure Sanguines will cry the hardest, weep the most often, throw the most violent temper tantrums, and pout the most frequently.

Yet their parents can rest assured that the Sanguine child is not on the verge of an emotional breakdown.

In the world in which we live today, the Sanguine is a survivor. There are very few things that can happen to Sanguines that will break them. A different environment will change even the worst things that happen in their lives.

For years parents have marveled at the Sanguine child. During the formative years they have worked very hard to develop a morally strong and well-disciplined atmosphere, only to have their grown children revert to behavior that should have been broken prior to adulthood. For the Sanguine this is typical. When the disciplined atmosphere or environment has ended, so has the discipline. In many cases, when the strict moral code of ethics has ended, so has the morality. Sanguines are very weak-willed people and, of all the temperaments, they are most likely to take on the morals and behavior of the people around them. This is so they can assure themselves of being accepted. Sanguines find it almost impossible to deny themselves. If there is something in their lives they believe to be theirs, they find it almost impossible to give it up.

Bad behavior is very hard for them to walk away from, especially if they believe they have a right to that behavior. The way to motivate a Sanguine is with love, attention and acceptance. Of all the temperaments, the Sanguine is the most responsive to praise, adoration, and love. However, if Sanguines can continue to receive love, attention, and acceptance no matter what their behavior is, they will not give up the bad behavior.

As we have already seen, the relationship to God and Jesus is an interpersonal relationship. The following information will help you understand how this interpersonal relationship is normally established. The pure Sanguine is normally introduced to God and His Son Jesus either through church, friends, or associates.

The first step for the pure Sanguine is to develop the desire to associate with God in which the temperament need in Inclusion must be met. Because the Sanguine is attracted to the more serious stabilizing person he or she must view God as serious and stabilizing and yet wanting full interaction with the Sanguine. His Son, the Lord Jesus Christ, must meet the same criteria. Yet there are other criteria that must be met: adoration, acceptance and attention. If the Sanguine perceives these qualities to be within the realm of God the Father and Jesus, then the Sanguine will let the relationship go further. If these needs are not met, the Sanguine will not allow the relationship to continue. This relationship will be on the surface at best, and they will not let God into their spirit.

Once the Sanguine has allowed the relationship to deepen, then the temperament needs in Control must be met. This person will still have pendulum swings and, if the Sanguine believes that God will allow him or her to be self-indulgent (as long as it is not sinful), then the relationship will go further. If the Sanguine is told or believes that self-indulgence is sinful and not allowed, then the interpersonal relationship is stopped.

Once God the Father and Jesus are allowed into the Affection area of the temperament and the Sanguine can interact with them in a deep personal relationship, then the change in the spirit and soul can begin. For the Sanguine to interact freely with God and for the Sanguine to receive Jesus, he or she must receive an abundance of love, joy, and peace.

Affection must be exchanged freely and in abundance; Sanguines must feel that they are loved and accepted. The threat of hell is of little use in the Sanguine's life. Death and hell are downbeat, and the Sanguine has little time for that. The threat of future punishment is too far removed from the present to be of any meaning to the Sanguine.

Major Temperament Needs Of The Sanguine

1. To be the center of attention and not be rejected.

2. To be provided with love, affection, and approval.

3. To have social interaction.

4. To find life situations where they can remain active.

5. To find life situations where they can interact with people.

6. To seek employment where they can undertake tasks while interacting with people.

7. To be accepted. When this individual is in the independent mode, i.e., self-gratifying and self-indulgent mode, they need to receive approval and not be "put down" for their indulgence.

8. To have recognition for the services they render.

9. To receive approval for their hard work and good behavior. They need to be pampered when they have taken on responsibilities and decisions.

10. To be self-indulgent (in accordance with God's Word) when they are in their dependent mode.

11. To make decisions and take on leadership when they are in their independent mode.

12. To receive physical expressions of love, e.g., touching, hugging, etc.

13. To be told every day they are loved and appreciated.

Special Things That Significant Others Can Do For The Sanguine

1. Tell them every day that they are loved, needed, and appreciated.

2. Recognize their need to socialize and provide them ample opportunity to do so.

3. Never reject them.

4. Provide them with large amounts of physical expression of affection. Touching is very important.

5. Give them recognition for all achievements and services rendered, perhaps by pampering them occasionally. They are motivated by the promise of reward.

6. Do not condemn them for being self-indulgent, providing they are not entering into an area of sinning against God.

7. Do not interfere with them when they have taken on areas of responsibility, and render assistance only when asked.

What Sanguines Can Do to Help Themselves

1. Learn to recognize anger as anger, and deal with it constructively and in ways pleasing to God.

2. Find life situations where they can interact with people frequently, especially in regard to employment.

3. Find life situations, such as a children's choir director, where their needs for love and affection can be supplemented.

4. When forced into life situations where they are away from people, they can lessen their anxiety by talking on the telephone, watching television shows about people, or reading books about people.

5. Listen to the radio or television while undertaking tasks. This will cause them to have a feeling of interacting with people, reducing their anxiety and increasing their efficiency.

6. Learn to anticipate the end results of their words and actions. This will help lessen their impulsiveness and emotional outbursts.

7. Learn not to adopt bad behavior and immorality to gain attention from significant others in their life. They will be jealous of the time significant others in their lives spend with other people.

8. Receive numerous expressions of physical affection, such as hand-holding, hugging, kissing, etc.

9. Learn to interact with God and Christ as they would in any other surface relationship, in order to lessen anxiety when they are forced to be away from people.

10. Go to Christ to receive the love and affection that is not provided through human means. This will reduce their penchant for sexual sins.

11. Learn to fulfill responsibilities. Sanguines in Inclusion tend to be somewhat irresponsible when it comes to completing tasks.

Behavior Changes That Bring Sanguines Closer to God

1. Learn to predict the end results of words and actions according to the ordinances of God.

2. Learn to deal with anger constructively and in ways pleasing to God.

3. Learn to become secure in the love of Christ to raise self-perception and to lessen their fear of rejection from man.

4. Learn ways to be self-indulgent that bring pleasure and are pleasing to God.

5. Learn to make their behavior pleasing to God and learn how to be accepted for good behavior. They will adopt the morality and behavior of the crowd to assure acceptance.

6. Learn to interact with God as they would any other surface relationship to lessen anxiety. They will suffer anxiety when they are forced to be away from people often or for long periods of time.

Conclusion

As you can see after completing this in-depth review of the Sanguine's behavior patterns and his or her temperament needs, it is important to understand why Sanguines do what they do and the causal factors of their behavior.

Even though we have taken such a deep and concentrated look at the Sanguine, it must be understood that this is not the absolute totality of the Sanguine. There are many additional needs and problem areas in the Sanguine, but they are minor compared to the ones that we have mentioned in this chapter.

Drs. Richard and Phyllis Arno

The Supine

❧ 17 ❧

Introducing the Supine

If you have ever heard of the Supine temperament, it had to be through the teaching and reportings of the Arnos. All other writers and researchers have concluded that there are only four temperaments. In 1984 the Arnos identified a fifth temperament. After several years of research this temperament type was named the Supine and introduced to the Christian community by the Arnos, the authors of this book.

Definition

The dictionary definition of Supine: is "Lying on the back or with the face turned upward." Some dictionaries go on to say: "Having no interest or care, inactive, negligent, listless." It must be noted that the Arnos choice of the name Supine is based only on the first definition of "Lying on the back or with the face turned upward." In fact Supines do have many interests and cares, although they do not express them. Supines are not inactive, although they are slow-paced and diligent. They are neither indifferent nor listless. Even with the noted differences in definitions, there seems to be no other word in the English language or any words translated from either Greek or Hebrew better suited for this particular temperament type.

Even though this definition refers to the physical posture, it perfectly describes the emotional attitude and temperament traits found in the Supine. Picture a servant slightly bowed before a king. The Supine is a bowing temperament, seeing everyone else as valuable and themselves as nearly worthless. Supines picture themselves as the individuals who were placed on this earth to serve others. They are our "Marthas" who work diligently in the kitchen to serve those whom they admire so much.

As you can see by this definition, the behavior of a Supine is so unique and different from that of a Sanguine and all of the other temperaments that it demanded a type classification of its own. Some authors have identified behavioral traits that could not be placed with any of the four original temperaments. However, they were unable to collect enough data and evidence to actually conclude that there is a fifth temperament. Some of these authors simply referred to these behavior patterns as "passive Sanguines." The fact is that they are so unique and different from the Sanguine that it is extremely misleading to refer to these people as Sanguine, whether passive or not.

The Melancholy temperament does not express a need for assertiveness in any area. For example, Melancholies do not express a desire for social interaction because, in fact, they do not want social interaction. They do not express control because they do not want to control others. And they do not express affection because they do not want affection.

Sanguines, on the other hand, expresses in all three temperament areas, and they want exactly what they express. The Supine "wants" the same as the Sanguine; however, Supines do not express their needs. In other words, they have the same needs as a Sanguine but look and act like Melancholies. Because of this indirect behavior, it might be said that Supines are their own worst enemy. They carry an unspoken sign boldly declaring "I DO NOT WANT" when in fact they want and need very much. They do not receive in the areas of Inclusion, Control, and Affection as no one knows of their need because they behave so indirectly.

The fact is, the Supine and the Sanguine have very little in common except their high need for love, affection, and approval. Their responsive needs, desires, and behavior patterns are significantly different.

Any study on temperament would not be complete without a comprehensive review on the Supine.

Supine in Inclusion

This section covers the temperament needs for social interaction, surface relationships and intellectual energies.

Supines in Inclusion are relationship oriented and need to relate to other people.

The Supine in Inclusion is both introverted and extroverted. This means that Supines express themselves as an introvert and respond as an extrovert. Because this person is quiet and usually found in the background in a social situation, the Supine appears to be distant and respond only when approached by others. Supines will not send messages that they want to be accepted nor do they assert themselves.

They want others to guess their need to socialize. They are often frustrated in their loneliness.

Supines in Inclusion relate to and understand tasks as well as they do people. When at parties or social activities, you would never guess from outward signs that they desire to be included. If the people around the Supine do not interact with him or her with acute sensitivity, the Supine will forever remain in social isolation.

The Supine Temperament can undertake numerous tasks, especially if these tasks are performed for the development of friendships. A person with this type of temperament can be extremely accommodating to other people, even at his or her own expense. The need to serve others and make them happy leads to Supines being natural born victims.

It is important to understand that the Supine in Inclusion wants and needs social acceptance very much. However, Supines view themselves as worthless, assuming they are neither wanted nor needed. They are totally dependent on others to recognize their needs and break down all the barriers by personally inviting them with an insistence that "we need you." If the insistence is viewed as genuine, then Supines will participate like a Sanguine.

When others do not "read their minds" and provide them with the genuine invitation needed, Supines in Inclusion will become very angry. Supines in Inclusion do not view themselves as angry but regard it as being "hurt." Supines in Inclusion seldom, if ever, admits they are angry. However, they will tell you that "their feelings have been hurt." This anger is normally manifested by withdrawal into self as a means of protection from further rejection and pain.

Supine in Inclusion Strengths

In the area of Inclusion, Supine strengths include a great capacity for service, liking people, and the desire to serve others. Supines possess an inborn gentle spirit.

Supine in Inclusion Weaknesses

The Supines' Inclusion weaknesses include indirect behavior that expects others to read their minds, high fear of rejection, and harboring anger viewed as "hurt feelings."

These temperament traits are present in each person who is a Supine in Inclusion, regardless of his or her Control and Affection areas.

Supine in Control

This section covers the temperament need for decision-making abilities, willingness to take on responsibilities, and the need for independence.

The Supine in Control cannot independently make decisions nor take on responsibilities. If forced to do so, Supines in Control become extremely anxious and insecure because they feel inadequate and worthless and are fearful of being left alone or having to take care of themselves. They are constantly searching the world for someone to take care of them. This does not mean that either the male or female Supine in Control is a weak person. On the contrary, Supines in Control are very strong. The fact is, no other temperament keeps and follows "the rules" any more than the Supine. They are totally incapable of "writing the policy." However, they are extremely strong when it comes to "enforcing" it.

Supines in Control want to be included in the decision-making process, and if they are not asked their opinion, they become very angry. They need to feel they are an important part and are respected. However, Supines in Control do not want to make the final decision and bear the responsibility. Supines in Control would rather be passive than be forced to take some kind of action. Therefore, they are constantly putting the responsibility for their lives in the hands of others.

Of all the temperaments, the Supine in Control internally harbors the most anger. There are two primary reasons for this anger. First, Supines are often excluded in the decision-making process, not being asked their opinions, and made to feel worthless. Second, they are angry because they live in a world where they are expected to "stand on their own two feet," and yet they lack the self-confidence and strength to make decisions and take charge of their own lives. Men suffer far more anger than women and are more apt to vent this anger both physically and verbally.

Motivating this person to do something is very easy. You need only threaten them with punishment. Your displeasure is enough punishment to move them. The person with the Supine in Control is extremely weak-willed, wanting to say "no" but not knowing how. So Supines in Control go through life doing all sorts of things they do not want to do for people. They begin feeling used, anxious, and angry. The person who is a Supine in Control almost always feels powerless and at the mercy of others, for, in essence, they are.

Other temperaments view the Supine in Control as a dominating type of person because their words and actions do appear dominating. However, they are only attempting to manipulate others into taking care of them.

The world is not kind to the Supine in Control, either in childhood or adulthood. When Supines are children, other children abuse and torment them, knowing they will be the last to fight back. Once they become adults, Supines in Control are again abused and tormented. This time it is by the more dominant, aggressive temperaments who order them around and dominate them in cruel, overbearing ways, until the Supine is overwhelmed with anger and anxiety. At that time, Supines in Control will turn on the people who have dominated them. The more dominant temperaments end up resenting this person almost as if they want this person to take a stand or fight back to get the respect due them.

Supine in Control Strengths

The strengths of a Supine in Control include dependability, ability to enforce "the policies" set by others, and to serve those they follow, their caretakers, with absolute loyalty.

Supine in Control Weaknesses

The Supine in Control weaknesses include aggressive disorders, open dependence, defensive against loss of position, weak willpower, difficulty in saying no to self and others, tendency to feel powerless and at the mercy of others. Supines in Control need others to make and be responsible for their decisions. However, they definitely become angry if their "choice" or "preference" is denied or opposite decisions are made by those in control.

These are the temperament traits that are present in each person who is a Supine in Control, regardless of his or her Inclusion and Affection areas.

Supine in Affection

This section covers the temperament need for love and affection, and the need for deep personal relationships.

Supines in Affection suffer from an "indirect behavior conflict" by expressing very little need for love and affection and appearing not to want deep personal relationships. In reality, they need a great deal of love, affection, and approval and they desire deep personal relationships. Because of their indirect behavior, people around them, who are unable to read their minds, are unaware of their intense needs. Therefore, the Supine in Affection is usually frustrated and unfulfilled because his or her deep affection needs are seldom met.

The Supine in Affection will definitely respond to love, affection, and approval AFTER the other person initiates it and fears of rejection have subsided. However, as stated above, the other person seldom shows initiative because the Supine in Control has sent a strong "signal" indicating that he or she neither wants nor needs this love, affection, and approval.

Supine in Affection Strengths

In the temperament area of Affection, the Supine strengths include the ability to respond to love and to open up emotionally when they feel emotionally "safe." If treated properly, Supines in Affection are capable of absolute and total commitment to deep personal relationships.

Supine in Affection Weaknesses

In the temperament area of Affection, the Supine weaknesses include the inability to initiate love and affection. Supines in Affection require constant reassurance that they are loved, needed, and appreciated. Yesterday's assurance means nothing. Actually, reassurance received one hour ago means nothing. Others are expected to read their minds and they become angry, which is defined by them as "hurt" feelings, when affection needs are not met.

These are the temperament traits that are present in each person who is a Supine in Affection, regardless of his or her Inclusion and Control areas.

The Supine Relationship to God

The pure Supine in Inclusion, Control, and Affection is capable of having an excellent relationship with God. This is particularly true if they were raised in a Christian home which offered the security of strong Christian discipline coupled with the teaching that God loves and accepts them and that this love was demonstrated by God in that "He first loved us." This assures the sense of acceptance and provides the foundation for a continuing relationship.

Even if the pure Supine is not raised in a Christian home, the possibility of becoming devoted to God is still very strong. Certain steps need to transpire.

The first step in interacting with God is in the area of Inclusion when the Supine is introduced to God. Since Supines in Inclusion are a responders and not initiators, when they come in contact with an inspiring preacher they will respond to his words. If Supines attend a church where they are welcomed and accepted, but requiring very little effort on their part, they will keep coming to church. If the preacher can give them the message of a God who welcomes them without much outward effort on their part, Supines in Inclusion will develop a deeper relationship with God. They seldom respond to "general" announcements and invitations to church functions; they must receive a "personal" invitation before attending church functions. Supines in Inclusion assume that general invitations do not include them since "they are worthless" and have nothing to offer.

After the Inclusion need is met, the Supine's need in the area of Control must be addressed. For the Supine, this need is usually easily met because of the traditional teaching of the church. If the Supine is taught that God is the absolute authority and that Jesus is the Shepherd who leads us and will direct our life if we ask Him, then the Supine will be able to yield to God in the area of Control. Since the Supine appears to be almost incapable of making decisions alone, the church must show him or her how to go to the Lord for conviction and correction when making decisions and taking on responsibilities. Supines must be taught to let God share their responsibilities and their decisions and learn how to talk and listen to God. If these needs are not met, then the relationship with the Lord is permitted to go no further. If these needs are all met, then the Supine will begin to seek a deep personal relationship with the Father.

In the area of Affection the Supine begins to have a deep personal relationship with God because he feels God's love, joy, and peace. If Supines understand that God loves them regardless of their feelings of worthlessness, then Supines will begin seeking God for a deep personal relationship. In this area Supines in Affection are the best of all temperaments for serving God. They love to serve and be supportive of deep personal relationships, but they do this because of the recognition they receive for that service. When it comes to serving God, Supines in Affection will work "their hearts out." However, if they are not taught how to see and understand the recognition God gives us in both this life and the next, then service to God stops. If Supines are not recognized for the service they give to the church, then that relationship is allowed to go no further. In fact, the Supine is the temperament that will actually become angry if he or she is not given that recognition or if it is given to someone else. This anger will be allowed to build up for only a certain length of time, then Supines will lash out. When they lash out, not only will they allow God no more input in their life, but they will actually turn their backs on Him, thus destroying the already existing relationship.

The pure Supine whose life belongs to God is one of the most precious people on earth. Without this relationship, however, their attempts to meet their unmet needs can be devastating.

The anger which the Supine shows is different from that of other hot-tempered temperaments. This anger is seldom seen by the outside world and is usually not even recognized as anger by the Supine since he or she refers to this anger as depression and hurt feelings. Nevertheless, these feelings are anger that is drawn and kept inside. The result of this may be an emotional outburst of explosive behavior. The murder mystery that states the "butler"did it is the story of the faithful Supine who served his master well for many years, felt used, and eventually reacted with murderous rage. This is an extreme situation that shows you how the Supine can react when pushed to the limit. In most situations, Supines will let this anger build until they turn away from the deep personal relationship that hurt them. Once that happens, that deep personal relationship will have a difficult time being restored.

Major Temperament Needs Of The Supine

The following is a list of the basic needs of a person who is a Supine in Inclusion, Control, and Affection (commonly referred to as a pure Supine).

1. To be included.

2. For others to be genuine.

3. To serve others. Supines do not demand acknowledgment of their service, however, they become angry if credit is given to another.

4. For others to initiate social interaction.

5. To be consulted (included) in decision making. However, Supines do not want to be the final decision maker.

6. To feel appreciated.

7. To receive love and affection. This needs to be expressed constantly — yesterday's assurance means nothing today.

8. For their deep relationships to initiate affection, e.g., touching, hugging, etc.

Special Things That Significant Others Can Do For The Supine

1. Tell them every day in words and actions that they are loved, needed, and appreciated.

2. Try to understand their needs to socialize and provide them with the emotional support to do so. Supines are not initiators; therefore, significant others need to initiate socialization.

3. Work very diligently to raise their self-image by reinforcing the positive and downplaying the negative.

4. Help them make decisions, take on responsibilities, and share responsibility for the decisions they do make.

5. Do not force them to act independently very often or for long periods of time.

6. Never force Supines to be the disciplinarian of the family.

7. Encourage them to give their input and state their preferences.

8. Encourage them to be more assertive in sharing the things that make them angry.

9. Accept their dependency without dominating them.

10. Give Supines recognition for the service they perform. They respond to both the threat of punishment and the promise of reward.

What Supines Can Do To Help Themselves

1. Try to develop a deep, personal friendship with someone (preferably the Lord) with whom they can share decisions and responsibilities.

2. Find employment or an environment where they can undertake tasks while interacting with people.

3. Try to discover life situations where they are not forced to take on too much responsibility or perform as leaders but rather function in supportive roles.

4. Learn to recognize their anger as anger and to deal with it constructively.

5. Learn how to be more assertive and to confront when confrontation becomes necessary. Supines need to voice their needs and desires.

6. Provide themselves with situations where they can supplement their needs for love and affection by seeking more friends, social interaction, and a deeper relationship with the Lord.

7. In order to diminish their anxiety and stress, learn to initiate telephone calls and read books or watch television programs about people.

Behavior Changes That Bring Supines Closer To God

1. Learn to deal with anger constructively and in ways pleasing to God.

2. Raise their self-perception by learning to see themselves as a wonderful, loved creation of God. This will make the fear of rejection from man less intense.

3. Learn to lessen anxiety by interacting with God and Christ as they would any other surface relationship.

4. Learn that God is always with them and will take care of them in order to lessen their fear.

5. Learn that manipulation through emotional blackmail supersedes the will of God.

6. Accept love and affection from God and Christ to supplement what they do not receive from human means. This will help prevent sexual sins.

7. Learn to seek direction in making decisions from God and Christ. This will strengthen their will power.

Conclusion

As you can see after completing this in-depth review of the Supine's behavior patterns and his or her temperament needs, it is important to understand why Supines do what they do and the causal factors of their behaviors.

Even though we have taken such a deep and concentrated look at the Supine, it must be understood that this is not the absolute totality of the Supine. There are many additional needs and problem areas in the Supine, but they are minor compared to the ones that we have mentioned in this chapter.

The Phlegmatic
❧ 18 ❧

Phlegmatic in Inclusion

This section covers the temperament needs for social interaction, surface relationships, and intellectual energies.

Hippocrates linked the Phlegmatic with phlegm, a body fluid that is thick, slow-moving and almost stagnant in nature. To the observer, the Phlegmatics are extremely slow-paced and stubborn. They allow their lives to become stagnant because it takes too much effort to use their talents. This person goes through life doing as little as possible, quietly, and expending little energy. It is not clear whether this is because Phlegmatics in Inclusion have very little energy, or if it is because they refuse to use what little energy they do have. The daily routine of the Phlegmatics is to go to work, sit in a cubbyhole and work with figures all day, go home, take a nap, eat, take another nap, and go to bed. They still have trouble getting up in the morning. This is extremely difficult for the family of a Phlegmatic. There is little energy left for the family by the end of the day.

Since Phlegmatics in Inclusion have no temperament needs to meet, they are nearly impossible to regenerate. The Sanguine in Inclusion regenerates through socialization, and the Melancholy in Inclusion regenerates through quiet time alone. However, the only thing that will even begin to regenerate a Phlegmatic in Inclusion is sleep, and that is often ineffective.

The world will never know how many brilliant thoughts, great books, beautiful works of art, or wonderful ministries died with the Phlegmatic. Phlegmatics in Inclusion never use these ideas and talents because it requires too much energy and active participation to put these ideas into action. The Phlegmatic sits back and watches other temperaments busy doing things wrongly and looking at all the things in this world that need to be changed. Identifying injustice is not difficult for Phlegmatics in Inclusion; however, they will never initiate action against this injustice. Based on their observations, Phlegmatics will try to inspire other people to do something. However, they will seldom get involved themselves.

The Phlegmatic temperament is task-oriented with a great capacity for work that requires precision and accuracy. Phlegmatics in Inclusion make great data processors, bookkeepers, librarians, accountants, records technicians, or museum curators. A writer may regard a Phlegmatic in Inclusion as the best person to catalog and do the research.

In social interactions, Phlegmatics are quite flexible and well rounded, even though they have no need to interact. Hence, the Phlegmatic in Inclusion can be either task-oriented or relationship-oriented, depending upon the situation. Phlegmatics in Inclusion have a dry sense of humor and, without smiling, at times can be quite humorous, even though it drives other temperaments crazy. Their dry, wry humor protects them from becoming too socially involved with other temperaments.

Phlegmatic in Inclusion Strengths

In the temperament area of Inclusion, Phlegmatic strengths include the ability to perform tedious tasks and to relate to both tasks and people. Phlegmatics in Inclusion are calm, easy-going, extremely efficient and perfectionistic.

The Phlegmatic in Inclusion can function quite well in a hostile social setting. Nothing "ruffles their feathers."

Phlegmatic in Inclusion Weaknesses

In the temperament area of Inclusion, the Phlegmatic weaknesses include unwillingness to become involved, tendency to be an observer rather than a participant, and use of a verbal defense that often hurts others.

These temperament traits are present in each person who is a Phlegmatic in Inclusion, regardless of his or her Control and Affection areas.

Phlegmatic in Control

This section covers the temperament needs for decision-making abilities, willingness to take on responsibilities, and the need for independence.

In the area of Control, Phlegmatics are an extremely well-rounded individuals who need only moderate control over the lives and behavior of other people, and they will accept only a moderate amount of control over their own life and behavior. When Phlegmatics in Control are self-righteous, they are nearly impossible to change, regardless of the circumstances. They are difficult to motivate, but they appear equally motivated by punishment or reward, or by the positive things that happen in their life as well as the negative. Phlegmatics in Control also appear to be very indecisive because they procrastinate. It is unclear whether the Phlegmatic in Control is indecisive by nature or because he or she is just naturally a slow mover. This indecisiveness could come from the fact that Phlegmatics in Control are very practical, down-to-earth people, or simply because making a decision takes too much energy.

Phlegmatics in Control are the most stable temperament. They have no real problems with the anger, rejection, or destructive emotions of the other temperaments. They have no compulsive needs or wants and suffer very little from bitterness or unforgiveness. The most damaging thing about Phlegmatics in Control is their stubborn resistance to change and their uninvolvement in life. Phlegmatics in Control are the most stubborn of all temperaments when it comes to making changes. The harder you push them to make changes, the more stubborn they become in resisting these changes. To change takes energy; to stay the same does not. Therefore, the Phlegmatic will take the path of least resistance, which is to remain the same.

They are natural negotiators and diplomats. Uninvolvement, while being a handicap for other temperaments, is a great plus for them. "Peace at all costs" is their motto. Therefore, Phlegmatics in Control have an uncanny ability to negotiate peace between two warring parties without becoming involved in the conflict.

The Phlegmatic temperament is the only one who can handle the Choleric, but the Choleric has no way of handling or controlling the Phlegmatic. Their "humor" leaves the Choleric so angry they walk away from the situation. Phlegmatics in Control use this humor to actively deal with the Choleric and to keep the Choleric from pushing them into doing something they do not wish to do. This wry sense of humor also protects the Phlegmatic from being inspired by the Sanguine or getting caught up in the self-sacrificing Melancholy. Phlegmatics in Control will accept the service of the Supine as long as they do not need to do anything in return.

Training materials for Christian counselors and A.P.S. reports (which are generated from the Arno Profile System Response Form) constantly refer to the Phlegmatic as having a "dry or wry" sense of humor which is defined as "quick comeback remarks." For example, if you were to tell a Phlegmatic in Control that he/she should trade automobiles, they would most likely "come back" with something like, "Yeah, I will run right out and buy a new car and send you the coupon payment book." Another example might be, "Wouldn't that be convenient? I buy the new car and you get to drive it!"

Phlegmatics in Control use their verbal abilities as a defense mechanism. Sometimes this defense mechanism is humor. Other times it can be very sarcastic and harsh. Their response depends on your approach and what you are trying to motivate them to do.

Phlegmatic in Control Strengths

In the temperament area of Control, the Phlegmatic's strengths include the tendency to be very practical, conservative, peace-loving, and a good peace maker/arbitrator.

Phlegmatic in Control Weaknesses

In the temperament area of Control, Phlegmatic weaknesses include indecisiveness, the tendency to procrastinate, and being very difficult to motivate. Phlegmatics in Control use verbal defenses that often hurt others. This verbal defense is used against anyone who tries to motivate or control them, particularly Cholerics.

These temperament traits are present in each person who is a Phlegmatic in Control, regardless of his or her Inclusion and Affection areas.

Phlegmatic in Affection

This section covers the temperament need for love and affection, and the need for deep personal relationships.

In the area of love and affection the Phlegmatic is the

most stable of all temperaments. Phlegmatics in Affection do not smother others, nor are they coldly distant. They can show a moderate amount of love and affection, and have very realistic demands when it comes to how much love and affection they need and the number of people from whom they need it. The Phlegmatic has no fear of rejection and can handle unaffectionate or hostile people. Phlegmatics in Affection are calm, easy-going people who are not plagued with emotional outbursts, exaggerated feelings, anger, bitterness, or unforgiveness as are other temperaments.

Phlegmatics in Affection deal with deep relationships as they do with most other things in their life. They are observers who do not get involved nor expend much energy. Their cool, complacent attitude can hurt the people that love them. The way Phlegmatics in Affection observe people can cause them never to give of themselves and, therefore, never receive either. Others involved in deep personal relationships with the Phlegmatic may have a very lonely life. This is because the Phlegmatic does not expend much energy to make or keep the relationships going. If any energy or sacrifice is necessary, it will most likely be done by the other people in their lives.

The Phlegmatic in Affection is unemotional and hates conflict, so when friends or family become angry, the Phlegmatics either ignore the anger, coolly observe the participants, or use their dry senses of humor to anger the other temperaments. A sense of self-righteousness causes the Phlegmatic to ignore what he or she is doing wrong, and Phlegmatics in Affection stubbornly refuse to make many changes. They are very happy just the way they are, even though the people who are involved with them are not as happy.

Phlegmatic in Affection Strengths

In the temperament area of Affection, Phlegmatic strengths include being well-balanced, easygoing, non-demanding, calm, and having realistic demands for love and affection.

Phlegmatic in Affection Weaknesses

In the temperament area of Affection, Phlegmatic weaknesses include unwillingness to become involved in deep relationships, tendency to be an observer only, rarely self-sacrificing, unemotional and unexpressive. Verbal defenses are used to protect low energy supply with regard to physical and sexual involvement.

These are the temperament traits that are present in all people who are Phlegmatic in Affection, regardless of their Inclusion and Control areas.

The Phlegmatic Relationship To God

The pure Phlegmatic in Inclusion, Control and Affection, is an observer. Phlegmatics observe life, relationships, and God. They allow relationships with others and God to pass them by. It is difficult for Phlegmatics to acknowledge God in their lives because they never really let Him become Lord.

God begins to work in the life of a Phlegmatic by introducing him or her to His Word through the church or a minister. This is not really a difficult task, for Phlegmatics will most likely listen just to keep peace. In church, they will sit back and observe the people around them to see how they are dealing with spiritual matters. Phlegmatics think they know what everyone is doing right and what everyone is doing wrong. Phlegmatics will listen to the preacher talk about some of the things that can keep people out of Heaven, such as lust, adultery, vengeance and fornication, and wonder what the fuss is about. Since these sins require too much energy, Phlegmatics are not really guilty. However, just to be on the safe side, they open their lives to God.

Phlegmatics understand that God wants changes, but the stubborn Phlegmatics will fight this. They justify their stubbornness by telling themselves they are all right just the way they are and, therefore, will make no changes. This leads to self-righteousness, which is a tendency to view everyone else as flawed and themselves as perfect. This may lead a

Phlegmatic to become self-satisfied in his own life, but it causes serious damage to his family and spiritual relationships.

When the Phlegmatic enters into a deep personal relationship with the Lord, he or she will neither demand nor give much. It is almost impossible to inspire Phlegmatics to do much for God. They will continue to drift through life, resisting God's efforts to work deep in their lives. They will appear to be nice, easy-going people who do all the things no one else wants to do. Phlegmatics will be the peacemakers who show the more volatile temperaments how to work together. They are the people who go about doing their work in a quiet, efficient manner and have no problems with sin. This person's noninvolvement with God is, in itself, a sin and he or she may not have undergone any meaningful spiritual changes in his or her life.

This temperament is unique in spiritual matters for they have no concrete temperament needs that must be met or compulsions that drive them.

When other temperaments sink to their weaknesses, Phlegmatics become miserable and make the other people around them unhappy.

Major Needs Of The Phlegmatic

The following is a list of the basic needs of a person who is a Phlegmatic in Inclusion, Control, and Affection (commonly referred to as a pure Phlegmatic).

1. To undertake tasks with a minimal amount of interaction with people.

2. To be free from excessive social demands.

3. To protect their low energy reserve.

4. To find employment which is methodical (research, record keeping, etc.) rather than physically demanding labor.

5. To have a peaceful and tranquil environment.

6. To share responsibilities and decisions with others.

7. To rest frequently, e.g., afternoon and early evening naps.

8. To make decisions without being pressured and to have all the facts. Phlegmatics are independent and do not like to be pressured by others. They are also very stubborn once they have made a decision.

9. To have only moderate demands placed on them with regards to romance and affection. Phlegmatics want and give very little affection.

Special Things That Significant Others Can Do For The Phlegmatic

1. Do not force them to socialize. People drain their energy reserves.

2. Share decisions and be willing to accept part of the responsibility for the consequences.

3. Show them they are loved and appreciated by using only a moderate amount of physical attention and doing special things for them.

4. Do not force Phlegmatics to take on full responsibility for someone else.

5. Understand their limited energy reserves and do not push them beyond that level.

6. Find special ways to keep them involved in deep personal relationships.

7. Be the aggressor in deep relationships.

8. Do not become angry and hostile because of their unwillingness to initiate affection.

9. Recognize that their wry, cutting sense of humor is only a defense mechanism to protect themselves and their low energy levels.

10. Do not attempt to force them or pressure them. They are self-motivated and do not respond to the threat of punishment or the promise of reward.

What Phlegmatics Can Do To Help Themselves

1. Find employment where they can undertake tedious tasks without being required to interact with people for long periods of time.

2. Maintain a proper balance of diet, exercise, work, and relaxation to insure proper energy balance.

3. Learn to show deep, tender feelings in ways that are comfortable and others can understand.

4. Be inspired to do something about the injustice they see.

5. Be inspired to stay involved in lives.

6. Be inspired to stay involved with the deep personal relationships in their lives.

7. Set activity guidelines to keep from sleeping their lives away.

8. Control their critical attitude about others.

9. Be more willing to make sacrifices for others.

10. Learn to be more flexible and less stubborn.

Behavior Changes That Bring Phlegmatics Closer to God

1. Learn to interact with God and Christ as they would any other surface relationship.

2. Learn to inspire themselves to do something about the injustices they see.

3. Learn that submission to God unlocks potential.

4. Learn to inspire themselves to be more open and loving with the Lord.

5. Learn to make decisions according to the Will of God and look to Him to defend them.

6. Learn to submit to the Will of God in order to lessen stubbornness.

7. Learn that only through expending energy and becoming deeply involved with personal relationships can they reach maturity. Phlegmatics have a tendency to deal with their personal relationship with Christ in the same way they do any other deep relationship, being spectators and not getting too deeply involved.

8. Learn to see the rights and feelings of others according to the Word of God. Phlegmatics will unthinkingly make humorous remarks about the rights and feelings of others.

9. Learn to depend on the opinions of God, not the opinions of people.

Conclusion

As you can see after completing this in-depth review of the Phlegmatic's behavior patterns and his or her temperament needs, it is important to understand why Phlegmatics do what they do and the causal factors of their behavior.

Even though we have taken such a deep and concentrated look at the Phlegmatic, it must be understood that this is not the absolute totality of the Phlegmatic. There are many additional needs and problem areas in the Phlegmatic, but they are minor compared to the ones that we have mentioned in this chapter.

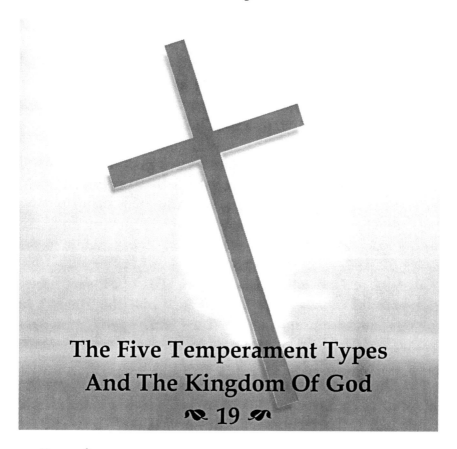

The Five Temperament Types And The Kingdom Of God
ᔏ 19 ᔒ

We have seen how the five temperament types are responsible for the distinction of the individual. Every individual is unique and has gifts and abilities that God has provided, through spiritual genetics, in order to build His Kingdom in heaven and on earth.

The first step in inspiring any person to receive Christ is to help him or her to see the need for salvation. There is no better temperament suited to this task than the Sanguine. The world's best evangelists and preachers are Sanguines. These charming, inspiring, personable individuals are able to bring the Word of God into the hearts of people in all situations. These optimistic, upbeat showmen, with words filled with fire and emotion, can bring thousands to their knees while the audience is in awe. Sanguines have the ability to inspire; and the charisma of their countenances can soften the hearts of even the toughest of temperaments. By the end of the sermon, many have taken Christ into their hearts. Many Christians owe their salvation to the Sanguine who inspired them, but those with a mature walk with Christ know this is only the first step.

These "baby" Christians are very susceptible to carnality and turning away. They need a very patient person who will help them reach their potential and Christian maturity. The Sanguine has become bored and is already moving on to the next stage and cluster of people, leaving these infants to the wiles of Satan. This is the reason the Lord has provided the Kingdom of God with Melancholies. These self-sacrificing, rich-natured people have the patience and the intellect to answer questions and teach. They will spend countless hours and sacrifice themselves to help the infants reach adolescence.

There is still much work to be done in the Kingdom of God. There are churches to be built, funds to be raised, Christians to be encouraged into service, and thousands of new projects to begin. The Lord has provided the best of all temperaments for this—the Choleric. This temperament is best at starting ministries, building churches, and encouraging other people to complete new projects. The Choleric who is totally committed to Christ is as inspiring as the Sanguine. With charisma and strength of will, Cholerics can build churches and head nationwide ministries. They have the capability of raising funds to develop and maintain these projects, all of which are done in the military fashion with which the Choleric undertakes all of their endeavors. Many fulfilled Christians owe their newfound service to the expert positioning of the Choleric who has found the perfect spot for them.

Within these worldwide ministries there are jobs that receive very little applause or attention. The Sanguine is not capable of handling these jobs due to his or her need to be the center of attention. The Melancholy is not suited for these jobs because they are not intellectually challenged. Who is going to keep the books, process the data, handle the mailings, and do the other jobs that require precision and accuracy? The Phlegmatic! Phlegmatics are the best people for this job. Bookkeeping is their forte, and the precision and accuracy with which they keep the books or accounts will astound other temperaments. They are the best suited to do the research for the Melancholy, keep the personnel records for the Choleric, and arrange tours for the Sanguine evangelist. The works of art and music that must be cataloged and the volumes of paperwork to be completed are all done by the Phlegmatic. You can see that the Phlegmatic has a special place that no other temperament can fill.

The Supine's position within the Kingdom of God is unlike any other, and no one else can fill it. A person who is a Supine has a great capacity for service, and when these temperaments are energized by God's Spirit their capacity for service is almost limitless. The Supine is very good at caring for the needy, visiting nursing homes and shut-ins, and serving people. In fact, Supines can undertake almost any task where they can serve people and receive recognition for that service. Supines will never tire of building a deeper relationship with Christ through service; however, they do need recognition for this service.

Even though these interpretations of temperament placement are over-simplified, you can see that temperament is important for understanding the individual. The five temperaments and the thousands of blendings of those five temperaments account for the placement of individuals and the work to which God has called them.

Drs. Richard and Phyllis Arno

Understanding Human Behavior
When Temperament Needs
Are Out Of Balance
❧ 20 ❧

Man attempts to meet his own temperament needs by fame, fortune, and power, but there remains a void that can only be filled by God.

When God is invited in, He brings new values and purpose. In other words, God will bring the temperament into balance.

Through spiritual knowledge and research, it is evident that balance can be interrupted if man is not taught exactly what his temperament needs are and how they must be met. All of us have some very basic needs that must be met if we are to remain at peace within ourselves, our environment, and with our God. A person's physical, emotional, and spiritual parts are affected if only one need is met and the others ignored. In this part of the book we will discuss what happens to human behavior when temperament needs are out of balance. In other words, how will the person's physical, emotional, and spiritual parts be affected if he/she meets one or two of the temperament needs and excludes the others?

The basic physical needs of the human that must be met are for food, shelter, liquids, and rest in the form of sleep and relaxation. If none of these needs are met, the human will suffer physical breakdown and eventually death. If one or two of the needs are met, ignoring the others, man will suffer physical breakdown and death.

The emotional side of man also has needs that must be met if emotional breakdown is to be prevented. These are the needs for socialization and association with other people (Inclusion), to have power and control over others or for others to have power and control over them (Control), and deep personal relationships and love and affection (Affection). If one or two of these needs are met while ignoring the others, the person will suffer emotional breakdown.

The spiritual side of humans must establish and maintain a relationship with God, who gives order and meaning to life. The needs within the spiritual side of humans are also in groups of three. The person's behavior must change when allowing the Word of God to govern his or her life. People must pray or meditate on the rules that God provides so that they understand them and worship God. If one or two of these needs are met, while ignoring the others, then the person will suffer spiritual breakdown or death to the soul.

Until recently, these three areas (physical, emotional and spiritual) were written about and dealt with separately. It was almost as if we did not understand that humans are also a creation of order, and, like all other creations, laws govern our unity. We contend that humans are a creation of order.

The order is this:

Physical, spiritual, and emotional. All three dimensions are present in all of us. If we are to be the best we can be, all three of these need areas must be met in a balanced way. We must understand that when these areas are out of balance, with one or more of them being ignored, all the other areas will be affected.

The steps to provide this balance are as follows.

Step One:

Keep yourself in the best possible physical condition:
a. For your age.
b. For your physical dexterity.

Step Two:

Develop a method whereby the temperament needs of Inclusion, Control, and Affection are met. These needs are met in three ways:

a. Change of environment
b. Change of thinking processes
c. Acceptance of one's unique temperament

Step Three:

Develop a relationship with God:
a. Read the Word of God.
b. Worship and pray.

This will free you from willful sin and make your life pleasing to God.

For the most part, humanity has never been able to totally understand the binding process of these three areas.

The physical side has been written about and researched over the years by the medical community with little understanding of the emotional or spiritual sides. This has prevented us from receiving needed help. However, many skillful, well-educated physicians know where the treatment of ailments are lacking, and they find themselves trying to understand and treat all three areas: physical, emotional, and spiritual. This has been especially beneficial in the treatment of patients who are terminally and chronically ill.

Humanists have been mostly responsible for understanding the emotional side of humans. Many of their theories explain our behavior. Because humanists have neglected to acknowledge that humans are created spiritual beings and that we must follow the rules, regulations, and order provided by God, they have neglected the physical and the spiritual areas. This has not given humanity a balance nor provided cures for the problems that have plagued mankind.

The Church has long recognized the needs of the soul and has filled this void with the knowledge and truth of God and His Son, Jesus Christ. Yet the Church has not recognized how the emotional and physical sides have a bearing on the spiritual development, therefore, providing no balance in man's life.

These different factions of society have dealt with the three different sides of humans, but they have not been able to cure the ills of humanity so that humans can be the best that God has created them to be. Each of these factions understands humanity by a different set of rules and regulations.

To give you a better understanding of how these areas work together, let us look at one of the problems humanity now faces which is threatening to destroy our world and our lives.

Alcoholism is one of the problem areas. Statistics show the seriousness of alcoholism and the number of problem drinkers. Watching local television shows gives you some of the information that is needed. There is a chain reaction to this problem that is found in all three areas of humanity. First, individuals have emotional problems that result in internal stress. This internal stress prevents them from coping with the world, thus heightening this stress. Because of this stress, sinful behavior and emotions may block them from the love, joy, and peace of God. Spiritually, they can no longer experience the healing power of God for they do not know what is needed or how to achieve feeling better. They know this is sinful behavior and they try to overcome it because the stress and pressure will eventually cause their deaths. They may believe drinking alcohol is a solution because media attention indicates that it is. They may know other people who deal with their problems in this way. Thus, they drink socially, progress to binge drinking, and then suffer bouts of drunkenness. Alcohol is a drug and, when taken in excess, causes physical changes and physical addictions in humans. Soon they will get to the point where the need for alcohol is ruling their behavior and drinking will be the driving force in their lives. The more they drink, the more they deny their physical, spiritual, and emotional well-being.

They plummet downward toward complete destruction. By the time alcoholics seek help, they are at the bottom and the rise to the top is a difficult and arduous journey. If they go to the medical community, they will receive help for their physical addiction and may well spend time on the emotional, but little is done with the spiritual.

The Church may tell them to repent of their sin and walk away from it. This nurtures their spiritual side, but does nothing for the physical addiction, nor does it help them to understand how their emotional needs must be met. Therefore, they are not able to reach the optimum that God allows.

This chain reaction is seen in many of the problems that now face humanity: adultery, fornication, lust, sexual addictions, depression, marriage disintegration, child abuse, spousal abuse, drug addiction, homosexuality, and many others. Although these studies are in their infancy, the facts and figures continue to confirm that there is a direct link between the non-fulfillment of temperament needs and many of the problems that plague humanity today.

Humanities Reaction To Unmet Needs

What would happen if people spent all of their time eating and sleeping without having their other needs met? The results are predictable. They would die.

Suppose individuals have spent all of their time reading the Bible and praying but did not apply what they have learned to their lives. What happens if they worship but do not read or pray? The outcome is predictable. They would suffer spiritual breakdown and spiritual death.

These simple rules of logic have been applied to the meeting of the temperament needs. If the individual's needs are met for Inclusion but their need for Control and Affection are denied, they will suffer emotional breakdown. If they spend all of their time meeting their need for Inclusion and Control, they will also suffer emotional breakdown.

Since the emotional sides of individuals are linked to and will react with their physical and spiritual sides, then, when emotional temperament needs are not met, it will affect the physical and spiritual sides of them.

To provide the foundation for spiritual growth and physical well-being, we must understand the temperament and provide a means to meet all the needs in ways which are healthy and pleasing to God.

In actual temperament studies, we have seen how this loss of balance works. For example, take a person who is a Sanguine in Inclusion, Supine in Control, and Melancholy in Affection. Because a person who is a Sanguine in Inclusion spends most of his or her time trying to meet his or her need for Inclusion, the other two temperament needs will go unmet. A person with this temperament blending will spend so much time trying to meet his or her need for socialization and association that he/she will neglect the need for the deep personal relationships that will help him or her make decisions and share responsibility for the decisions he or she does make. People with this temperament blend will also neglect the need for those few personal relationships within their temperament needs. This happens because they spend so much time going places and surrounding themselves with large numbers of people with whom they want to socialize, and they do not spend the time necessary to develop those deep personal relationships that are needed.

After a short while, these persons will begin to feel the sinful and destructive emotions of anxiety, depression, loneliness, and loss of self-worth. They will feel unloved. These emotions will bring about some very specific and significant physical changes, such as a loss of weight, stomach ulcers, high blood pressure, fatigue and other stress-related ailments. These people know they do not feel well, but they do not know why. They deal with these emotions the only way they know how, through socialization and association, but now the effort is more frenzied for they feel worse than before. At this time the temperament weakness will begin to come into play.

Since Sanguines will adopt the morality of the crowd and undertake whatever behavior is needed to be accepted, they will be more driven to be accepted and liked. Their behaviors will become worse, which will add to the feelings of loss of self-worth and not being loved. Now they cannot love themselves.

Yielding to the flesh (carnality) and state of sinfulness will come next, for Sanguines will feel unworthy even for God's love. Sanguines will feel that they cannot receive redemption from these sins. This will add to the emotional and physical breakdown.

The circle is complete and the downhill slide may accelerate.

In this case, the temperament needs were denied, which caused the physical and spiritual problems. However, this case is not unique, for even if one of the temperament needs is not met the person will suffer emotional problems, physical ailments, and finally carnality.

A young woman who is a Melancholy in Inclusion, A Melancholy in Control, and Sanguine in Affection has no trouble in meeting her Inclusion and Control needs. She is an introvert and enjoys being at home with her children and husband and has only a few surface relationships with which she spends time. Her husband is also an introvert, so he is never forced to do things, go places and be with people. The two of them enjoy long hours at home reading books and watching television.

Her Control need is also being met for she is independent, and this independence is recognized and respected by her family and friends. They do not interfere in her chosen life style and do nothing to cause stress in the Control area of her temperament.

She is suffering temperament stress because her Sanguine in Affection demands deep personal relationships for love, affection, time, attention, and acceptance. She has no way of knowing this. Her husband is meeting part of her temperament needs for order, reliability, dependability, and responsibility. However, since only part of her temperament needs are being met, she will spend a great deal of her marriage feeling that her husband and her children do not love her.

Her husband loves her very much, but because he is emotionally guarded he rarely shows or tells her how he feels, which she desperately needs to hear. She also needs physical expressions of love and affection, but because of his temperament he does not provide these expressions. For short periods of time she can deny this temperament need, especially when she can keep her mind active and thinking of other things, but the longer the need for love and affection is not being met the worse she will feel.

This is especially true late at night or after everyone has gone to bed, for at these times she can no longer keep her mind active and the downward thinking process spins dramatically. She is unable to sleep until early in the morning when physical exhaustion takes over. When the alarm goes off in the morning, she is tired and does not want to face another day.

The lack of energy causes her to awaken already feeling depressed. Because of this feeling, she cannot deal with her children and her husband effectively. She is irritable, short-tempered, and not very pleasant to be around. Instead of seeing all the things her family does to show her love and affection, her mind will automatically focus and search for evidence that indicates they do not love her.

At this time, the emotions she feels are deep-seated anger, loss of self-worth, feelings of being unloved and unaccepted, anxiety, and loneliness. At night, when these feelings are intensified, she cannot sleep, which makes things worse. If she goes to a doctor, she will probably be diagnosed as being exhausted and receive a prescription for tranquilizers or sleeping pills to allow her body to receive the rest it needs. If she goes to a psychiatrist she may be diagnosed as deeply depressed and given an antidepressant drug. Neither of these will solve the problem, for the out-of-balance temperament needs remain unfulfilled.

The following things will probably occur because of her temperament. She will begin to read books that place her in another fantasy life, which will make her life seem all the more hopeless and lonely. At night, instead of feeling lonely and unloved, she will likely undertake romantic or sexual fantasies which, for that time, make her feel loved and accepted. Because of her Inclusion these fantasies will appear to be real. She can sleep at night, but in the morning she is still tired because now she hates the life she is living, for it cannot measure up to the perfect life she has in her mind. She may even find herself wandering off into these fantasies during the day when she should be concentrating on her family and husband.

Sinful emotions are now being intensified. She also feels guilt because she knows that these adulterous fantasies are allowing something to come between herself and her husband. Physical problems will range from simple fatigue to many stress-related ailments. Spiritually, she will no longer seek the will of God, for she knows in her heart that if she does this she will have to give up these fantasies and they are the only things that help her through the long and lonely nights. Therefore, she separates herself from God into a state in which she may remain for the rest of her life.

The progression of the study is simple.

1. A temperament need was not met because it was not recognized; therefore,

2. the unmet needs caused sinful emotions,

3. which caused physical problems,

4. which caused sinful behavior, and

5. resulted in separation from God.

The following is another example to help you better understand this concept.

A young man who is a Melancholy in Inclusion, Choleric in Control, and Supine in Affection is the most likely to undertake the sins of child abuse and spousal abuse when his temperament needs are out of balance. The reason for this is simple. The Choleric in Control is the power area. When a person has this Control, he or she spends most of his or her life trying to control and gain power over the people around him/her; thus, other temperament needs remain neglected.

This young man has only a few surface relationships that must meet his need for profit and power. He exerts pressure on these surface relationships, for they are weaker-willed persons. Eventually, they will begin to feel used and become angry at being manipulated. This anger will cause them to reject the young man, which will make him angry and feel rejected. He will feel a of loss of self-worth, unacceptance and that he is not being liked. The anger and vengeance he feels from these emotions will be directed at the only people left in his life, who are his family.

He will begin dominating his family unmercifully. He will need to use them, not only to meet his intense need for love and affection but also to meet his need for profit and power. The rejection of the surface relationships makes the temperament try to save face before the world, so he also places the family in the position of making him look good to the world. This is a heavy burden for them to bear.

Since he is a Choleric, all of these things must be done according to his terms. He will not accept anything his family does that conflicts with his preference. Soon they will feel as if they can do nothing right and they may as well stop trying, so they too reject him and will act only out of fear. During this time, the young man is undergoing physical changes, i.e., loss of appetite, high blood pressure, eating disorders, or any of the other stress-related ailments. Because he feels like this, he blames his family and he seeks vengeance for the feelings and the physical problems he is suffering.

At this time, his needs for love and affection are being completely denied. The driving force in his temperament is the need for control. The deep-seated anger begins to erupt in bouts of physical or emotional abuse, which drives his family further from him. He blames others for this deeper rejection. If they would only do as he says, things would be all right. Therefore, he seeks to punish them more to get them "on track." The bouts of physical violence or the emotional browbeating will become more frequent. From here, he will seek God to rectify the situation by bringing everyone under his rule to do as he says. When God does not do this, because He will not override man's free will he will turn his back on God and begin to beat his family into submission. From here the progression is predictable.

This example will give you a better understanding of why people can do the terrible things they do to the people they love. The Melancholy in Inclusion and Choleric in Control is the most angry of all temperaments, and while they are experiencing this anger it overrides all the tender emotions they feel, i.e., love, compassion, gentleness, peace, and joy. These emotions are lost beneath the feelings of anger.

In these examples, you will find that, when the temperament needs are not met, the person will suffer emotionally, then physically. Sometimes the progression of the breakdown will not be as severe. A person can suffer anxiety attacks and other emotional and physical problems when the temperament needs are not met.

Conclusion

The human being is made up of three specific areas. They are:

a. Physical
b. Emotional
c. Spiritual

Within each of these areas there are specific needs that must be meet. The needs in each of the areas must be kept in balance for the individual to remain at peace within himself/herself and his/her environment.

The major physical needs are:

a. Nourishment and drink
b. Shelter
c. Rest The major spiritual needs are:
   Relationship with God
   Reading the Word of God
   Prayer, worship and praise

To have meaning and order in our short lives, we must maintain a balance within our spiritual need areas.

The major emotional needs are:

a. Inclusion
b. Control
c. Affection

To be completely in balance, all three of the temperament needs must be met. If any of these needs are denied, the person will suffer emotionally, which in turn will cause physical and spiritual problems.

Since the human is made up of complete order, this order must be maintained in all areas of one's life.

This must be done in stages. These stages are:

Humans must have their temperament needs for Inclusion, Control, and Affection met.

Humans must maintain their best possible physical condition.

Humans must maintain a relationship with God and be freed from sin.

Drs. Richard and Phyllis Arno

Maintaining Balance In Inclusion, Control, And Affection

❧ 21 ❧

Many of the problems the world faces today are caused by man's inhumanity to man. This accounts for the numerous incidents of violence, thefts, cruelty, and abusive words. As stated previously, the most frequent sin that befalls man is the sin of selfishness. There is one more problem area that causes man to destroy himself and the people he loves, and that is when the needs of the temperament are denied. Man will react to unmet needs.

Temperament needs go unmet because they are not recognized or understood.

Throughout this book we have stated, and we feel it must be repeated, that the temperament need areas are Inclusion, Control, and Affection. To remain emotionally strong, these need areas must be met as prescribed by God within the parameters of the temperament.

The temperament is not only made up of needs but also made up of perfections which are called strengths and imperfections which are called weaknesses (man's reaction to unmet needs).

When the three temperament need areas are met and in complete balance, the individual is in unity and is less likely to fall into an area of temperament weakness. If the temperament needs are not met in all three areas, the individual is filled with internal stress, which makes him/her more likely to fall prey to the weaknesses of the temperament. These individuals will also fall victim to stress-related physical problems and "the flesh" (carnality).

The temperament needs can be met in three ways:

1. Change of environment
2. Change of thinking process
3. Acceptance of one's own unique temperament

To give you a better understanding of how this balance can be achieved, we will again look at the three previous temperament blendings and show you how meeting these needs will make a difference.

The first temperament blending we will discuss is the person who is Sanguine in Inclusion, Supine in Control, and Melancholy in Affection. This person is an extrovert and needs people, parties and going places to meet the need for Inclusion. This person needs to know of this need and strive to meet it, however it must be met (in a Godly way) so that the other needs will not be denied.

The need to socialize is the basis for attracting the deep personal relationships, which he/she must have, to share in making decisions and accepting responsibility for the decisions made. This ability to socialize is also an excellent device for attracting those very few deep personal relationships needed to provide love and affection. To accomplish this, this person must learn to limit the number of surface relationships developed to those who basically have the same morality and behavior he/she possesses. In this way, this person is better able to discover who will help make decisions and share responsibilities for the decisions made. This person will have the same beliefs as the Sanguine, and in this way the Sanguine's advice would be better pleasing to the Lord. This deep relationship's advice can be trusted and used.

When this person is surrounded with the people who share the same morality and behavior, he/she is better able to find those few deep relationships who will provide the love and affection needed and will respect his/her gentleness without domination.

People with this temperament blend limit social encounters and suffer anxiety. To overcome this anxiety, they must learn to do things when they are in isolation that will help them. Reading books or watching television shows about people and talking on the telephone will lessen this anxiety. However, these must be limited if these people are to meet their other temperament needs. At times, when all social encounters must be denied (for the sake of the other temperament needs), they must learn to interact with God as in any other relationship.

To prevent adopting the poor behavior of others, they must learn to conform their behavior and morality to standards pleasing to God and be accepted for their good behavior. If they are rejected or cannot attend some of the social functions because of these beliefs, then they must learn to accept God's attention and acceptance.

The temperament need for a deep personal relationship is a desire to share decision-making and responsibilities. People with this need must learn to love, trust and depend upon one of their deep personal relationships who will accept them the way they are. Even then there will be times when the friend is inaccessible, and they will feel anxiety and a sense of being lost. They must learn to see themselves as capable of making decisions and taking on responsibilities, freeing them to use the abilities God has given them and allowing them to be more responsible for their lives. Whenever they are not sure of what they should do or how to do it, they must learn to go to God to confirm all decisions and allow Him to share the responsibility for the decisions made. This will be less demanding of deep personal relationships and will prevent family and friends from feeling used and crowded. This allows others to better meet his/her needs for love and affection.

People with this temperament blend must learn to see themselves as unique, loved children of God. They have worth in the eyes of God. Once they know this, they are better able to accept the love of family and feel better about themselves.

In this example, this person went through therapy and made the changes needed to bring the temperament into balance. This not only freed the individual from internal stress, but provided a foundation to become one spiritually with the Lord. Now the person can learn how to be free from sin by accepting the Lord Jesus Christ as Lord and Savior.

We will now look at a second temperament blending. A young woman that is a Melancholy in Inclusion, a Melancholy in Control, and a Sanguine in Affection.

In this example, the woman is very dependent on the significant others in her life to help her meet her temperament needs. But she must first become aware of these needs and verbalize them. Since there is already a foundation of love, and respect, she can tell her husband what she needs and he can help her meet them. She needs a great deal of time, attention, love, and affection from the few people in her life. She also has a "skin hunger" that needs to be satisfied by touching, hand-holding, kissing, hugging, and other physical expressions of love and affection. She also needs to be told every day that she is loved, and because her needs are so much higher than her husband's she must find ways to supplement them. If she remains demanding of her husband, his temperament will be stressed and he will begin to feel as if his space is being invaded and he is crowded. He will withdraw from her because he finds her clinging to be quite repulsive because of his Melancholy in Affection. The ultimate therapy is to teach her husband about her need or love, affection, and approval and to obtain a commitment from him to give of himself in order to meet her needs. To overcome the anxiety that develops when her needs are not met through her husband, even if he is cooperative, she must find ways to supplement these needs. She must:

1. Learn to be more demonstrative (expressing her love) to the children and to her other family members.

2. Allow herself to do what comes naturally for her temperament—hug, kiss, touch, and tell them she loves them.

3. Feel free to allow them to do the same thing for her.

Even at best, with these changes there will continue to be times when she is filled with anxiety and loss of self-worth because she does not feel loved.

It is during these times that she must learn to recognize the loving things her family does for her by saying, "They do these things because they love me!"It is this simple process that will help her to feel loved. Even with these changes, she must:

1. Learn to relate to God in a way that will meet all of her temperament needs.

2. Learn that whenever she is lonely and feels she does not belong in a social environment, to see herself as a person of worth.

3. See all of the good things God has given her.

4. See God as a Being who is with her at all times and who will not reject or forsake her.

5. Know that she can interact with Him on a personal level at all times.

She must also see God as a Being who will provide her with complete freedom and independence, for no longer does she have to be controlled by the rules of family and friends. Now she need only abide by the rules that God has given her, which are easy to follow. By submitting to the will of God, she need not fear the unknown because God will guide her. By following Him into the unknown, she is then free from failure and criticism because God will protect her from both.

She must also learn to relate to God in a way that will meet her need for love and affection. This is done very easily. Anytime she feels lonely and unloved, she must learn to go to God and know that He will provide her with all the love and affection she needs. He will fill her to capacity with that love, and if she opens her heart fully to Him she can even feel Him holding and protecting her. This will make her less demanding of deep relationships. It will also help her feel loved at all times in her life. The temperament needs have been brought into balance, and this young woman has been taught to see God on a personal level, allowing her to be one with Him.

The last temperament blending we will discuss is a man who is a Melancholy in Inclusion, a Choleric in Control, and a Supine in Affection. This person must first learn to meet his need for Control in a way that is foreign to him. He must understand that he cannot control everyone and every situation, regardless of what he does, for God, even with His immense power, does not override a person's free will. Therefore, a person with this temperament must learn that

God can meet his/her need for profit and power. He can do so by allowing the people around him to feel good about themselves and the work they do. He can love them with the love that God has given him, encourage them, and give them genuine compliments.

Undertaking good behavior will prevent him from being rejected by surface relationships. It will also prevent the feelings of loss of self-worth. When others cannot meet his need for profit and power, he must learn to seek God to meet these needs. This can be done by dedicating all achievements and all he does to God and waiting for His blessings and His recognition.

This person must:

1. Learn to see profit, not in monetary gains but in what can be done to profit his soul and to live in light of eternity.

2. Learn to see power, not in the ways of man but in the ways of God, who determines his destiny in light of eternity. There is no greater power than this.

To meet his need for Control, this individual must:

1. Keep complete control over himself and his behavior. By doing this, he gains complete independence over his life.

2. Begin to see that the only way a man can have complete control and independence is when he will not allow the actions of others to determine his own behavior.

3. Know all things he does and says must be pleasing to God and to himself.

4. Realize this powerful Control area was not given
   to him to allow him to control everyone and
   everything. It was provided: To give him the
   strength of will to control himself. To allow
   him to overcome all of the obstacles that are placed
   in his way. To help him become all that God wants
   him to be.

This individual must also take responsibility for the environment he chooses. He needs an environment where his need for independence and achievement can be met and where he can use his ability to make decisions and to take on responsibilities without problems. He must never work or live where he is under the thumb of a strong authority. There should be areas in this person's life where he is free to do what he wants, when he wants, and be free from interference from others. When he finds himself in a position where he must submit to an authority, he must say to himself, "I am doing this because I choose to do it, because no one can make me do anything I do not want to do." This change of thinking process will allow him to feel free and in complete control of his life.

When he finds himself in a place where he cannot control or make others do what he wants, even if that is the right thing to do, then this person must learn to release those things to God for His final disposition.

To meet the temperament needs for love and affection, this person must learn to be more direct in showing love and affection to his family and friends.

In this temperament, the Law of Reciprocity holds true because this person shows much less love and affection than he needs. Therefore, his needs will not be met. To overcome this, he must:

1. Learn to show more love and affection so he can receive more love and affection.

2. Feel completely secure in the love of God and the love of his family.

3. See himself as a person worthy to be loved and to see all the things which God has provided.

God's love will be evident as this individual learns to see himself as a unique creation of God and loved by Him. He will be less fearful of rejection and better able to show others his need for love and affection instead of expecting others to meet these needs. This man must then learn to accept the love and affection initiated by others, saying to himself, "They are doing that because they love me and that is exactly what I want them to do — to love me."

Even with all of these changes, the Supine in Affection will cause him to feel unloved and unaccepted. During these times, he must learn to go to God to receive the love and affection he so desperately needs. He can do this in prayer. He must be open to the Lord to develop love, joy, and peace. He can do this anytime his need for love and affection is not being met through human means.

When temperament needs in all three areas are being met, it helps to control the desires and emotions that lead to sinful behavior. This affects stress-related physical problems.

Conclusion

The temperament is made up of three
specific need areas:

Inclusion, Control, and Affection.

The needs in all three of these areas must be met if
the person is going to remain physically, emotionally, and
spiritually in balance.

When one or more of the temperament needs are not
being met, such people will feel sinful emotions and desires
that will make them more likely to fall into the temperament
weaknesses that are caused by unmet needs. These weaknesses
make them more likely to undertake sinful behaviors, which
separate them from God.

Compulsive Needs Of
The Temperaments
~ 22 ~

A compulsive need is when the person is driven to meet that need without an act of will power. When a compulsive need exists within the temperament, a person will focus most of his or her attention and behavior toward meeting that need. Compulsive needs are unique in that they are almost impossible to meet without divine intervention. A compulsive need within the temperament is like any other compulsion. No matter how many times a person gives in to the compulsion, it can never be met or be satisfied.

Four of the five temperaments, Melancholy, Choleric, Supine, and Sanguine, possess compulsive needs in Inclusion, Control, and Affection. The Arno Profile System (A.P.S.) will reveal any compulsive need areas. The only temperament that has no compulsive need is the Phlegmatic.

Since a compulsive need cannot be met by earthly means or methods, each individual must learn to meet these needs through the intervention of Christ.

Compulsive Needs in the Area of Inclusion

The Sanguine compulsive is a person driven to socialize with people. It does not matter how many times compulsive Sanguines socialize or how many people they are with, they are constantly looking for new ways to socialize and more people to be with.

The Supine compulsive is a person who will appear to be shy and withdrawn in social situations but will also need to socialize regularly. Compulsive Supines, no matter how many times they are included or how many people they associate with, will never really feel accepted or wanted.

The Melancholy compulsive is a person who withdraws from social situations and associations. It does not matter how many times you prove yourself, this person will be distrustful and rejecting.

Compulsive Cholerics are constantly looking for people to associate with on the surface, yet they want to associate with almost no one. Those they associate with are people they can use, dominate, and motivate. It does not matter how many times they use people or how many accomplishments they undertake, it is never enough.

Compulsive Needs in the Area of Control

The Sanguine compulsive possesses the compulsive dependent/independent conflict swing. When needing to take on responsibilities and make decisions, a compulsive Sanguine's ability will astound people. No matter what he or she does, how well he or she does it, or how much recognition he or she receives, it will never be enough. The more compulsive Sanguines feel like this, the stronger the drive will be to become self-indulgent.

Likewise, when compulsive Sanguines are being self-indulgent, their self-indulgence is never enough or satisfying. In other words, they are miserable in their state of self-indulgence. They feel worthless and selfish. They become angry at themselves and begin imposing very strict self-control and self-discipline. In fact, this is the major part of their problem; they are overly self-disciplined and excessively strict in their self-expectations. They then swing from their excessive unfulfilled self-indulgence to unrealistic self-expectation and self-sacrifice.

Supine compulsives has a driving need to have others control them, take care of them, and help them make decisions. Their behavior, either good or bad, manipulates the people around them to meet this need. The more you help compulsive Supines make decisions and take on responsibilities, the less they will do for themselves.

The same is true for the recognition they receive. It will not matter how many times you say thank you. It will not be enough. They reach a point when they want recognition for even the simplest of tasks.

Melancholy compulsives fear unknown situations, of making fools of themselves, and of looking incompetent. They are driven to appear competent and in control. This compulsive need will prevent them from moving into the unknown and keep them fighting to maintain control over their lives without making decisions for other people.

When people have a compulsive need to look competent, it will never matter how well they do or how well the world thinks they are doing. They will never feel competent.

Choleric compulsives constantly look for people to dominate and ways to gain more and more profit and power. The problem is, no matter how much control they have over others, it will not be enough to satisfy this need. These people will focus most of their behavior on keeping control over the people, places, and things around them while allowing absolutely no one to control their lives.

Compulsive Cholerics have wills of iron, and as they gain more power over their environment, the more power or control they will require.

Compulsive Needs in the Area of Affection

Sanguine compulsives never feel completely loved and accepted. The more love they are shown, the more they need. Once the cycle is established, these people will show and demand much love and affection and begin to suffocate those around them. Still, they do not feel loved.

Supine compulsives are unable to apply the principle of reciprocity. This is why they never feel loved. These people show almost no love and affection; therefore, they receive very little love and affection. They appear to have little desire for love, but, in reality, they want unlimited love from a limitless number of people. Since they respond with the same needs as the Sanguine, it does not matter how much love they are shown; it is never enough.

Melancholy compulsives have both low introversion and low self-esteem. It is almost impossible to make them feel loved and accepted. They are compulsively distrustful of people and constantly look for reasons why they are being shown love and affection. Because of these traits, it is impossible for any human to make them feel loved and accepted.

Choleric compulsives never feel loved. They do not feel love because they are compulsively driven to mold, bend and browbeat the people around them into showing love and affection according to terms and standards. The people around them can never meet these terms and standards, therefore, the Choleric compulsive never feels loved.

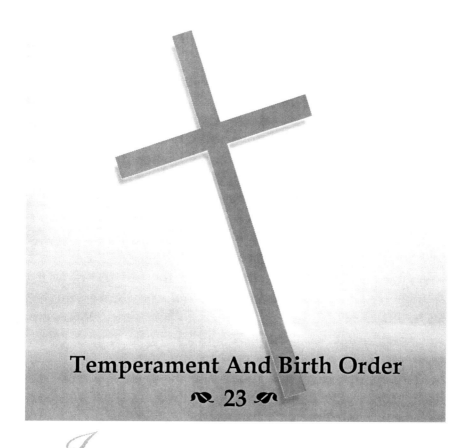

Temperament And Birth Order
❧ 23 ☙

It is very important to understand how birth order has a direct effect on the temperament.

Temperament is a "hands on" creation of God, what we are calling spiritual genetics. Since a person's placement within the family and the years that separate him or her and the other siblings are ordained by God, then this, too, is as much a part of temperament as the actual genetic makeup.

The differences in behavior attributed to birth order determine the way siblings see themselves, the expectations the parents place on them and the differences in the treatment of each child. These differences are universal within the working of the family.

The economic, religious, or ethnic background of the family do not affect the parents' expectations and the perceptions of each child. Even within troubled families, where there are instances of child or spousal abuse, these expectations are still present.

The effect of birth order on behavior cannot be measured or scored, but it can be understood. The birth order of the child has such an effect on the temperaments that the traits taken on by the child remain with him or her long after the child reaches adulthood and leaves the immediate family. In fact, the molding remains with the person until death. This molding and refining occurs within the person and has the ability to magnify strengths and heighten weaknesses.

This is especially true of the first born child. Usually when parents are expecting the arrival of the first born child, everything is new and exciting. From the pregnancy to the actual birth, their hopes and dreams for the future are wrapped up in this small child.

Beginning with the first word to little league, piano lesson to high school and college, children are pushed to be the best, smartest, and to achieve the most. If a child has the temperament that thrives under this kind of pressure, he/she will become an independent, perfectionistic person, always driving, always reaching for that illusive achievement that will fulfill that driving need. If a child has the type of temperament that cannot meet this challenge, he or she will still want to achieve and try to please someone. However, he/she will feel he/she never measures up.

By the time the middle children come along, the parents are "old pros." They know what they are doing and face this new life with confidence. The things this new child does, although a new experience for the child, were done first and probably better by someone else. This is a difficult situation for a young person in which to find himself or herself.

The middle born, if they have certain temperaments, will develop behavior traits completely different from the first born, always searching for a unique place for themselves. A serious child soon discovers it is easier to compete in the outside world, so he or she will go outside the family to develop both close personal and surface relationships. The more outgoing temperaments will also go outside the home; however, they will be more rebellious and less disciplined within the home.

What gives the middle child's position its uniqueness is that this child is left to develop his or her own temperament because of less interference from the parents in his/her life.

By the time the last child comes along, the parents have not only mellowed but they are tired. They are older and do not possess the energy reserves they once had, and this dwindling supply is split between the other siblings. Whatever this child does, it is not as exciting as it was with the older siblings. This child soon learns that, if he/she wants to receive time and attention, drastic action is required.

The problem of the last born child is made worse because his or her parents know this is the end of the line, so they discourage the child's maturing and leaving the nest. Without realizing it, they are encouraging this child to remain immature, selfish, and childish.

Because of the antics that last born children pull, they receive the time and attention of the parents. These antics will be determined by the temperament. A less serious temperament will pull antics such as being a clown, talkative, or undisciplined to get the attention of the parents. A more serious temperament will cling to the parents and deep relationships, barely letting them out of their sight or smothering them with closeness. Other temperaments will observe competing siblings and develop behaviors different from theirs, either good or bad, so that time and attention is assured.

Drs. Richard and Phyllis Arno

The Identification Of Behavioral
Patterns And Temperament Tendencies
☙ 24 ❧

Based on research conducted by the Arnos between 1983 and 1991, it has been determined that certain temperament types are more likely to commit violent acts or participate in habitual behavior.

Each of the following categories rates the pure temperament types in order from most likely (1) to be involved in the listed behavior to least likely (5).

Drug/Alcohol Abuse

1. Melancholies. They lack the ability to express emotions, and it is the only way to alleviate their pain.

2. Sanguines. They have a high need for socialization and a willingness to adopt the moralities of the crowd.

3. Supines. They lack self respect, have feelings of worthlessness, are unable to just say "no," and build up anger and frustration.

4. Phlegmatics. They need a peaceful atmosphere and avoid confrontation with a "peace at all cost" attitude. They may drink or take drugs as a means of escape.

5. Cholerics. They socialize for gain. For example, they may drink with clients to complete a sale or with the boss to get a promotion, etc.

Suicide

1. Melancholies. They tend to be very lonely and seldom open up to others. They rarely recover from the loss of a loved one, not just through death but any loss (divorce, job transfer, etc.). In addition, they are perfectionistic and struggle with the injustices of life.

2. Supines (particularly males). They suffer from pent-up anger and feelings of inferiority and worthlessness. However, suicide is usually a ploy for attention that turned "sour" (accidental suicide). To complete the act they need encouragement from someone telling them they should do it and how.

3. Sanguines. This is very unlikely because they have a "bounce back" attitude. If a Sanguine does commit suicide, like the Supine, he or she would attempt it only as a ploy for attention. Most Sanguines who commit suicide could be listed as "accidental suicide."

4. Cholerics. Very rare and only as a means of having the last word (for example, Hitler).

5. Phlegmatics. This would be the least likely of all because no situation would ever cause them to be that "upset." They are "lukewarm, middle of the road" people (unexcitable). They probably do not have the energy to carry it out.

Sexual Abuse (Molestation and Rape)

1. Melancholies. The tendency toward sexual abuse is usually "second generation," meaning the offender was first abused. If, as a child, the Melancholy was molested, he/she will probably molest others as a means of venting anger.

Melancholies have a difficult time forgiving and forgetting. They play it over and over again in their mind until they become obsessed with it. This obsession usually manifests itself in the violation of another person.

2. Choleric. The Choleric detests weakness, tenderness, romance, compassion, and any sign of emotion. Unless taught otherwise, Cholerics take what they want without remorse, guilt, or concern for the feelings or rights of others. Cholerics need a sense of power and control over the lives of others, and they are quite capable of rape and molestation as a means of expressing their power.

3. Sanguine. This one is very doubtful. Sanguines are lustful (skin hungry); however, they have a conflict. On the one hand, there is something in them that controls any desire to commit such an act, that is, the fear of rejection. On the other hand, if a Sanguine was with a gang who was doing this, he/she would participate because of the fear of being rejected by the gang members. In other words, a Sanguine would probably never do it as an independent act.

4. Supine. Supines, like the Sanguines, would probably never commit such an act independently. However, if Supines received enough peer pressure from "strong" or "controlling" friends, they would participate in "gang rape" because of their need to be included and accepted.

5. Phlegmatics. Never! No gang could pressure them because they are stubborn and independent. Besides, no individual could entice them enough to waste the energy.

Physical Abuse

1. Cholerics. They exercise their power and control over others and have a cruel, insensitive, intolerant attitude toward the emotions of others.

2. Melancholies. They act out of their vengeance and pent-up anger. In their minds, they see themselves physically hurting others (they play it over and over again, like a movie). By the time they actually commit a hostile act of physical violence, they do it with very little emotion, cold and calculating.

3. Supines (particularly males). Like Melancholies, they have a lot of pent-up anger. Supines are very giving and caring people; however, they must receive recognition for what they do. If you cross them or make them feel like they have been used, they can become very violent, both physically and verbally.

4. Sanguines. They have a difficult time controlling their temper. They flare up and often do things they soon regret. They seldom learn from their mistakes and often repeat poor behavior even though their remorse is real. Their instantaneous anger is normally vented verbally; however, if they learn to vent their anger in physical ways (the way their mother or

father did), they will probably do the same. In other words, the Sanguine will always express their anger verbally and, if they are physical, it is because they learned it from someone else.

5. Phlegmatics. Extremely doubtful. They seek the path of least resistance and love peace. Besides, physical violence requires too much energy.

Note
Keep in mind, the above listed tendencies are just that — tendencies. The actual behavior of a given individual may be affected by learned behavior, environmental necessities ("rough" neighborhoods, etc.), or other compelling factors.

Conclusion
1. Temperament is placed in us by God while we are still in our mother's womb. Observation of newborn babies indicates how differently each baby reacts to their environment. Some love to be held, some prefer not to be held, some cry a great deal, and some never cry. How we act and interact with our environment is called our temperament.

2. God has a perfect plan for each life, and He clearly uses our temperament as a means for guiding our lives. Example: If His calling and perfect plan for a person's life is to be a carpenter, He will give that person the temperament of one who enjoys working alone and is basically task-oriented.

3. You have been instructed in the importance of the temperament and how it affects our behavior. By now, you should have a functional understanding of the general behavior patterns of the five pure temperaments: Melancholy, Sanguine, Supine, Choleric, and Phlegmatic.

4. You have been taught that, even though two persons might have an identical temperament, their actual behaviors could be very different because of the effects of the environment (learned behavior).

5. You were taught that it is very difficult to correctly identify a person's temperament by observation. There are some general areas where it is clear what a person is. A Melancholy compulsive in Inclusion can usually be identified by observation. But for the most part, identifying temperament by observation is very difficult and often misleading.

6. You have learned that temperament needs must be met and that most inter and intra personal conflicts, which result in relationship problems, are a direct result of temperament needs:

> Not being met.
> Being met in ungodly ways.

7. We have emphasized that temperament does not simply "determine an individual's emotional needs." Temperament also determines how individuals react when their needs are not met. Recall that a Sanguine becomes nearly "insane" with anger and then totally forgets about the entire matter within ten minutes or so. A Melancholy will "simmer" for the rest of his or her life and will, at least in his or her mind, seek vengeance. A Supine "pouts." A Choleric is "going to win at all costs," and the Phlegmatic is not "ruffled" at all.

A Final Note

Our primary goal for providing this book has been to help you understand the mysteries of God's wonderful creation of the human race.

We pray that we have provided you with the knowledge of who God created you to be. We also pray that having this knowledge will aid you in developing and maintaining relationships with others, especially with the Lord Jesus Christ. You are created by God and you are a very special person. The Lord loves you and He has a wonderful plan for your life.

Special Offer

You can receive your own Personal Arno Profile System (A.P.S.) report. It is a 7-8 page profile which will accurately reveal your individual temperament in the areas of Inclusion, Control, and Affection — your spiritual genetics.

Please complete the information form below and mail it to:

S.A.C.C.
5260 Paylor Lane
Sarasota, FL 34240

Drs. Richard and Phyllis Arno

Request Form:

Name *(Please print all information)*   Telephone *(Daytime)*

Mailing Address,   Telephone *(Evening)*

City,   State,   Zip

Please mail the A.P.S. Adult Response Form to me. I want to receive my Personal Profile.

I am enclosing my personal check/money order, made payable to the S.A.C.C. in the amount of $39.

□ Please charge my □ Master Card □ Visa in the amount of $39

Card Number_____ Exp.____/____

Signature_____ Date_____

Additional Information

The Sarasota Academy of Christian Counseling provides a course titled Creation Therapy. This course is provided for ministers and laity who believe that God has anointed them and called them into the Ministry of Counseling. Persons who complete Creation Therapy and become members of the S.A.C.C. are certified to administer the Arno Profile System. The A.P.S. is extremely useful to counselors engaged in an effort to help others.

The National Christian Counselors Association provides courses for Christians who would like to be certified and/or licensed as a Pastoral or Christian Counselor. In addition, the N.C.C.A. has an excellent degree program and can assist Christians who would like to obtain their A.A., B.A., M.A. and/or Ph.D. degree(s).

For additional information regarding the training and services provided by these two educational institutions, please write to:

Drs. Arno
5260 Paylor Lane
Sarasota, FL 34240

Also, any comments regarding this book should be forwarded to the authors at the above address.

Glossary of Terms

Accountable: being responsible for your actions.

Affection: temperament area that indicates need for love and affection and need to establish and maintain deep, personal relationships with people. This includes physical demonstration (touching, holding hands, etc.) and emotional openness.

Aggressive: willing to engage in bold, direct behavior, sometimes at the expense of others.

Amoebae: a one-celled animal.

Anthropology: the study of mankind.

Arduous: difficult, requiring labor.

Assertive: confident and persistent in pursing goals, without denying the rights and feelings of others.

Attributed: belonging to, having a quality or characteristic.

Behavior: the conduct or activity of an individual.

Birth Order: the order in which children are born into their families.For example, first born, last born.

Carnal: "of the flesh"; worldly or fleshly.

Causal Factors: the specific parts that cause something to happen.

Choleric: One of the 5 temperaments that is characterized by a need to dominate/control situations, self and others. Also known for leadership capabilities.

Competent: able.

Complacent: easy going, neglectful.

Conducive: leading to or in agreement with.

Control: temperament area that indicates a need to establish
and maintain satisfactory relationships with people
in respect to power and control and decision making
abilities, willingness to take on responsibilities and
the need for independence.

Conviction: being convinced of something.

Craven: cowardly.

Creationists: people who believe that God created human
beings as they are, not evolving from lower life forms.

Defense Mechanism: any self-protective response.

Demonstrative: to prove, to show, make clear, show feelings.

Determining Factor: a specific part that causes or determines
something else.

Dichotomists: those who believe humans have only 2 parts
body and soul.

Differentiated: separated by differences.

Direct Correlation: when two events are directly related to
each other. For example, one event causes the other.

Dissertation: a paper written on a specific topic after detailed
research, usually as a requirement for a college
degree.

Distinguishable: to perceive clearly, recognize plainly, to
separate and classify.

Doctrinological: systematic teaching of a belief or idea as a fact.

Dominant: stronger/controlling.

Effectuate: to bring about, cause to happen.

Encompasses: includes, contains, to bring about, surround.

Endocrinological: medically dealing with the endocrine glands and internal secretions of the body.

Evolutionary Thinking: thinking based on the idea that humans evolved from a one-celled organism.

Evolutionist: someone who believes in the theory of evolution.

Excitatory: able to be excited.

Exhaustive Study: to completely investigate a topic, covering every detail.

Expressed Needs: a measurement of the innate ability of the temperament to express/demonstrate (physically and emotionally) their needs.

Extroversion: directing one's interests outside one's self; very expressive and outgoing.

Extrovert: one who is very expressive and outgoing.

Facilitated: made easier, helped, assisted.

Factions: parts or divisions.

Free Association: relationship of words and meanings bypassing one's defense mechanisms.

Habituated: something that has become a habit.

Hinder: to prevent or get in the way.

Histrionic: overacting, theatrical or dramatic display
of emotion.

Humanism: edification of self. The belief that humans can
solve their own problems through rational thinking
without the need for God. i.e.: that is to say (in other
words).

Illusive: unreal, having the nature of illusion. That which
causes misperception of reality.

Imperative: essential.

Impulsive: inclined to do things without forethought of
consequences, quick to act.

Inadequate: not sufficient, not able to do what is required.

Inclusion: temperament area that indicates a need to
establish and maintain satisfactory relationships with
people regarding surface relationships, association
and socialization. Also includes intellectual energies.

Indirect Behavior: acting or expressing one behavior but
wanting another. Expecting others to "read
one's mind".

Indulgence: the act of giving way to one's own desires.

Inferred: assumed, deducted.

Inhibited: held back, reserved, shy.

Inhibitory: holding back, prohibiting.

Initiate: to start.

Initiative: the will and desire to do start something.

Interpersonal: between persons, of or involving relationships.

Introversion: turned inside to oneself, inward.

Introvert: someone whose focus is inward upon themselves, opposite of extrovert.

Isolate: to separate and make alone.

Law of Reciprocity: as one gives, he/she shall receive. What one sows, he/she reaps.

Manifested: made clear or evident, proved, shown.

Manipulate: to manage or control skillfully, to use one's influence to gain a desired outcome.

Melancholy: one of the 5 temperaments that is characterized by a need to be alone, creative, independent, perfectionistic and rebellious.

Mishna Torah: the first part of the Talmud, the books containing the Jewish civil and religious law.

Motives: inner drives or intentions.

Narcissistic: excessive interest in one's appearance, self-worship.

Negotiators: people who are good at bargaining, conflict-resolution, and discussion.

Neurotic: having a mental dysfunction such as anxiety, compulsive behavior, or depression.

Nomothetic: based on law, a science of general or universal law.

Non-realization: failure to realize, oblivious.

Omnipotent Being: abeing that is all-powerful.

Omnipresent: able to be everywhere or present at all places at all times.

Omniscient: all- knowing.

Ordained: called by God and set apart for a specific purpose.

Ordinance: an established or prescribed practice, often believed to be a decree of God.

Penchant: a strong liking or fondness.

Perceive: to view or see something in a certain way.

Perception: the way one views a person, place or situation.

Phlegmatic: one of the 5 temperaments characterized by their slow pace, lack of energy and non-commitment to life.

Physiological: having to do with the physical body and its functions.

Plummet: something that weighs heavily, or to fall or drop straight downward.

Prerequisite: something that is needed before something else can take place.

Presupposes: assumes.

Procrastinate: toput off, postpone.

Psychological: having to do with the mind.

Psychology: the study of the mind.

Psychometrically: using tests to measure psychological variables such as intelligence, aptitude and personality traits.

Psychopharmacological: the study of the effects of psychoactive drugs on the mind and behavior.

Psychostatistical: amethod of research that compares the results of psychological profiles in order to create statistics.

Qualitatively: having to do with the quality or worth of something.

Quantitatively: having to do with the quantity or amount of something.

Recessive: pulling back, able to be dominated by a stronger force. Hidden or obscured.

Regenerate: refresh, renew.

Responsive Needs: a measurement of the innate needs of a temperament usually called wanted behavior, which may be unobserved, introverted.

Sanguine: one of the 5 temperament types characterized by extroversion. Out-going, people oriented, boisterous, extravagant, affectionate and a tendency to be irresponsible.

Sarcastic: cutting, biting, ironic.

Secular: having to do with worldly or non-Christian worldviews.

Self-gratifying: satisfying one's self.

Self-indulgent: giving way to the desires of the self.

Self-righteous: showing one's belief of being morally superior to others.

Significant Others: close relationships such as mother, father, sister, brother, husband, and/or very close friend.

Stagnant: not moving, stuck.

Submission: obedience, surrendering, or yielding to another's power.

Subservience: the act of being useful, helpful or serving.

Supine: the 5th temperament type identified by Drs. Arno. Supines are characterized by their indirect behaviors and inability to initiate. They are people pleasers who feel their only purpose is to serve others.

Susceptibility: the capacity or ability to be influenced.

Task-oriented: focused on accomplishing goals.

Temperament: the inborn part of man that determines how we react to people, places and things.

Tenets: basic parts or components of beliefs.

Terminally: having an end or finish.

Theologians: people who study God, the Holy Scriptures, and religion.

Therapeutic Classification: a type or category of therapy dealing with a specific method of treatment.

Thermodynamics: physics that deals with the relationships between heat and other forms of energy.

Transpire: to develop, to come about or happen.

Trichotomists: those who believe that humans have 3 parts: body, soul and spirit.

Triune: having 3 parts. For example, God the Father, Jesus the Son, and the Holy Spirit.

Typology: the study or systematic classification of types that have characteristics or traits in common.

Ultimate Reality: the spiritual part of man in communication with God achieving fellowship with Him.

Validity: ability to be proven as a fact, how true something is.

Volatile: explosive, having the potential to explode.

Volitional: having to do with the will.

Wiles: schemes or plans, usually for evil purposes.

Resources
⌐━━╍━╍

Adams, Jay E.; "Shepherding God's Flock," Michigan: Baker Book House 1984.

Allee, Ph.D., John Gage (Editor); "Webster's Encyclopedia of Dictionaries," Ottenheimir Publishers, Inc., New American Edition 1978.

Buss, Arnold H., Plomin, Robert; "ATemperament Theory of Personality Development," New York: John Wiley & Sons.

Carr, John C.; Hinkle, John E.; Moss, III, David M.; (Editors); Wise, Carroll A. (Foreword); "The Organization & Administration of Pastoral Counseling Centers," Nashville: Abingdon 1981.

Davis, John D.; "Davis Dictionary of the Bible," Michigan: Baker Book House 1978.

Eysenck, H. J; Rachman, S; "The Causes and Cures of Neurosis," California: Robert R. Knapp Publisher 1971.

Eysenck, H. J.; "A Model for Personality," New York: Springer-Verlag 1981.

Eysenck, H. J.; Arnold, W.; Meli, R.; "The Encyclopedia of Psychology," New York: Sebury Press 1979.

Gilliland, Glaphr'e; "When the Pieces Don't Fit... God Makes the Difference," Michigan: Zondervan Publishing 1987.

Kant, Immanuel, Trans. by Dowdell, Victor Lyle; "Anthropology from a Pragmatic Point of View," Illinois: Southern Illinois University Press 1978.

Kennedy, Ph.D., D. James; "Learning to Live with the People You Love," Pittsburgh: Whitaker House 1987.

LaHaye, Beverly; "The Spirit-Controlled Woman," Oregon: Harvest House Publishers 1976.

LaHaye, Tim; "Understanding the Male Temperament," New Jersey: Fleming H. Revell Company 1977.

LaHaye, Tim; "Your Temperament: Discover Its Potential," Illinois: Tyndale House Publishers, Inc. 1984.

LaHaye, Tim; Phillips, Bob; "Anger is a Choice," Michigan: Zondervan Publishing 1984.

LaHaye, Tim; "Spirit-Controlled Temperament," Illinois: Tyndale Publishing 1966.

LaHaye, Tim; "The Transformed Temperament."

Laymon, C.M. (Editor);" The Interpreter's One Volume Commentary on the Bible," Tennessee: Abingdon Press 1971.

Leman, Dr. Kevin; "The Birth Order Book," New Jersey: Fleming H. Revell Company 1984.

Meier, M.D., Paul D.; Minirth, M.D., Frank B.; Wichern, Ph.D., Frank; "Introduction to Psychology & Counseling, Christian Perspectives & Applications," Michigan: Baker Book House 1982.

Merrill-Palmer Quarterly, Vol. 26, No. 4, 1980, p 299. Morris, Ph.D., Ed. by, "Scientific Creationism," California: Master Books 1974.

Patterson, C.H.; "Relationship Counseling and Psychotherapy," New York: Harper & Row 1974.

Schutz, William C.; "The Interpersonal Underworld," California: Science & Behavior Books, Inc. 1966.

Strelau, Jan; Farley, Frank H.; Gale, Anthony; "The Biological Bases for Personality and Behavior," New York: Hemisphere Publishing Co. 1985.

Taber, Clarence Wilbur; "Taber's Cyclopedic Medical Dictionary," Philadelphia:

F.A. Davis Company (11th Ed.) 1969.

Thompson, D.D., Ph.D., Frank C. (Editor); "The New Chain-Reference Bible," King James, Indiana: B.B. Kirkbride Bible Co., Inc. 1964.

Wolman, Benjaman B.; "Contemporary Theories and Systems in Psychology," New York: Harper and Roe Publishers 1960.

Zondervan; "The New Compact Bible Dictionary," Michigan: Pillar Books for Zondervan Publishing 1977.

LaVergne, TN USA
17 March 2010
176282LV00009B/113/P